STRAND PRICE
5.00

DEDICATED TO
PETER V. ZARUBIN
&
S.C.

Published in 2003 by
Stewart, Tabori & Chang
A Company of La Martinière Groupe
115 West 18th Street
New York, NY 10011

Export Sales to all countries except Canada, France,
and French-speaking Switzerland:
Thames and Hudson Ltd.
181A High Holborn
London WC1V 7QX
England

Canadian Distribution:
Canadian Manda Group
One Atlantic Avenue, Suite 105
Toronto, Ontario M6K 3E7
Canada

Library of Congress Cataloging-in-Publication Data
Zarubin, Lora.
I am almost always hungry: seasonal menus
and memorable recipes / Lora ; photographs
by Tessa Traeger ; foreword by Jay McInerney.
p. cm.
ISBN 1-58479-287-6
1. Cookery. 2. Menus. I. Title
TX714.Z37 2003
642'.4--dc 21   2003054213

Recipes for Truffled Pork Crépinettes (p.160) copyright
© 1997, Thomas Keller's Vegetable Spoonbread in
Brioche Crust (p.174) copyright © 1996, and Oyster
Shooters with Tabasco and Ginger Vodka (p.181)
copyright © 1997 Conde Nast Publications. All rights
reserved. Originally published in *House & Garden*.
Reprinted by permission.

The text of this book was composed in Scala
Art direction and design by Anne Johnson
Edited by Gail Monaghan

Printed in Hong Kong

10 9 8 7 6 5 4 3 2 1

First Printing

I am almost always hungry

SEASONAL MENUS AND MEMORABLE RECIPES

LORA ZARUBIN • **PHOTOGRAPHS BY TESSA TRAEGER**

FOREWORD BY JAY MCINERNEY

STEWART, TABORI & CHANG • NEW YORK

TABLE OF CONTENTS

REMARKS

FOREWORD Jay McInerny

It seems entirely appropriate that I first became acquainted with Lora Zarubin through her cooking. For an all too brief spell in the late eighties, Lora's, in the West Village, was one of my favorite New York restaurants, although I don't recall that I ever met the proprietress. At the time, downtown restaurants were divided into those places where you went to see and be seen and those places where you went for the food. (We won't speak about the tourist traps.) Although Lora's had a surfeit of celebrity patrons, the food was the real draw. It was a homey place and the menu was startlingly simple at a time when chefs were competing to see how many diverse and incompatible ingredients they could cram into one dish, when every meal seemed to be topped with something along the lines of raspberry chili cilantro vinaigrette with green tea anchovy sorbet. Ah, yes, the eighties. Who can remember them? Strangely enough, I do remember a sublime grilled chicken I had upstairs at Lora's. When I first saw the menu, I didn't know what to make of it, so devoid of frills and flourishes. Where the hell was the chipotle mango pesto? (When I later learned she was from San Francisco and was friends with Alice Waters of Chez Panisse fame, the whole thing made a little more sense.) Over the course of a few visits, I noticed that the menu changed almost daily and was based on seasonally available ingredients.

I was very sorry when Lora's closed, despite excellent reviews, but not necessarily surprised—that kind of low volume, artisinal operation could not have been terribly profitable. Years later I met the proprietress in the Grill Room of the Four Seasons in Manhattan where we had both been invited for lunch by our mutual friend Dominique Browning, the new editor in chief of *House & Garden* magazine. Lora had just been hired on as food editor and Dominique was entertaining the admittedly eccentric idea of hiring me to write a wine column. Lora was there to check me out. I got the distinct impression that, although she had never met me, she believed every bad thing she had ever heard and read about me. Of course, to give her credit, I'd just crawled out of bed after a rough night and was not, as we say of certain wines, showing very well that day. For my part, I thought she could have been a little more open-minded and sensitive to my hangover. I know that good chefs are supposed to be temperamental, but still . . . a great friendship did not seem pre-ordained.

Seven years later we have spent hundreds of pleasurable hours together (and more than a few unpleasant ones when we were lost and exhausted and sick of each other on some byway in Provence). It is a reflection of Lora's passionate belief that food and wine are inseparable companions that has resulted in our working and traveling together. I've come to enjoy my role, riding shotgun and puzzling over Michelin maps as Lora races from winery to cheesemaker to backroad remote country trattoria, driving like a bat out of hell in search of the next ecstatic revelation. Of course, for every discovery there are several disappointments, and a few days of this kind of quest can be exhausting. But at the end of a long day in a long week, Lora will drive an extra hundred miles chasing down a rumor of wild boar salami. I've been waiting for this book for many years. Often when I find myself expecting guests I call Lora for last minute advice. I'm an enthusiastic cook, but not a terribly knowledgeable or skillful one—and I'm always amazed at the way she comes up with a meal that's simple enough for me to prepare on relatively short notice and which subsequently astonishes and delights my guests. Halibut in parchment with salsa verde? Sounds pretty exotic, but it only takes an hour to make, as you will discover in these pages. Lora has convinced me that if you get the freshest, highest-quality ingredients—you can make something that Mario Batali and Emeril Lagasse could hardly improve upon. One of the things I've learned while being dragged through farmer's markets from Union Square, New York, to Portland, Oregon is the importance of careful shopping, of finding sources for the freshest fish and produce, the oldest, most flavorful dry-aged prime beef. Being a good cook, according to Lora, starts with being a good shopper, which involves going with the flow of the season and the region in which you find yourself. It also involves buying a few basic pieces of equipment, which will do half the work for you.

I am familiar with most of the dishes herein, having eaten them at Lora's apartment in Chelsea or been present when the seed of a recipe was planted in Chianti or Marseilles or Calistoga. Dining at Lora's table is one of the great pleasures of my life. It's a total aesthetic experience, from the old linens and silver she scavenges at flea markets to the food—all this in an apartment that measures less than 800 square feet. Dining out with her, if not always as wonderful, is always instructive—a kind of bacchanalian seminar. Unlike some epicureans of my acquaintance, Lora really loves to eat and, as she says, she's almost always hungry. So far as I can tell, if she has a fault, culinarily speaking, it's her disdain for goat. So don't expect any good cabreo recipes here.

Simplicity has become something of a mantra in recent years as Mediterranean cooking and bistro food have overshadowed classic French cuisine. Lora's been there for years. I am a great fan of master chefs like Daniel Boulud, Alain Ducasse, and Thomas Keller (as is Lora), but their cookbooks kind of scare me. I don't for a minute believe that I can create at home the kind of meals that I pay these guys to make. That's why I keep going back to Daniel and Ducasse and French Laundry.

A few birthdays ago, Lora presented me with a Tuscan grill for my fireplace—one of the most useful presents I have ever received. Cooking over fire is one of the most primal human experiences and is a central technique in Lora's approach to cooking.

In our travels, Lora is always looking for food, which is local and authentic. In France, she tends to look for the one-star restaurants (on the Michelin three-star scale) believing them to be more likely to reflect the home cooking of a region. She is fierce in her disdain of overly tricked-out food. I once spent a very tense three hours with her at a two-star restaurant in Avignon. Her indignation grew to the bursting point as we ate one over-sauced and regionally anomalous course after another and I was terrified when the chef came out to ask us how our meal was—fortunately she kept her real opinion to herself. I often have to act as the diplomat in these situations. Lora seems to feel that bad food is a crime against humanity. These perfectionists can be difficult to live with.

But when Lora finds what she considers the genuine article, her rapture is unbounded. She literally chortles over a simple tomato soup with thyme at the unstarred Mas de Turturon in Gordes, for instance, where we shared a perfect meal in the courtyard of an old farmhouse surrounded by birdcages hanging from the trees. After a *carne crudo* in the Piedmont region of Italy she hugs the chef. In Alsace she pledges lifelong friendship to Olivier Humbrecht and his wife, Margaret, after eating fresh white asparagus with speck (a regional ham) and enjoying a 1990 Humbrecht Muscat at the picnic table outside their home.

Lora will travel any distance for a good meal. We once flew to Strasbourg and then drove four hours south to eat an all-cheese dinner at Bernard Antony's Fromagerie in the tiny village of Vieux Ferrette. All told we tasted some fifty different cheeses, and perhaps half as many wines, Lora frequently bursting into some enthusiastic exclamation, half French and half English, as the evening progressed, taking copious notes all the while. Although Mr. Antony speaks no English, and Lora's French is rudimentary at best, she manages to make herself perfectly understood at moments like this, when she is excited about a new food or wine discovery. I find it nothing short of miraculous. All of these culinary expeditions have, one way or another, made their way into this book, which I suspect will soon become the most bespattered and dog-eared cookbook in my own collection.

The most important thing I have learned from Lora is that a big heart is the essential ingredient in cooking and entertaining. The rest will follow, particularly if you keep this book close to the stove.

INTRODUCTION A word from the cook

Whenever I think about where my love of food began, I go back to my memories of being a little girl in San Francisco sitting in church on Sunday mornings. Since we are Russian, we would usually attend two services, one in English and one in Russian. That was the hard part. The good part was the great meal that followed the long, long service. As soon as the wonderful smells began rising to the pews from the kitchen below, I would start to daydream about what the women down there were making. The only real praying I did in church was for pelmeni, a dumpling in chicken broth that is a little like a ravioli. Before long I was fantasizing about how my food would look on the plate and what I would eat first. My stomach would growl and often I would eat a box of Luden's cherry cough drops to stop the hunger. My greatest hope was that the Holy Spirit would be too tired that morning to inspire a long sermon from our enthusiastic pastor. As soon as the service was over, and while everyone else was greeting neighbors, I was downstairs in the kitchen inspecting our meal and trying to get a little morsel of something to taste. From a hungry, curious child I have become an adult who is still almost always hungry for new experiences, tastes, and discoveries.

In my family, good food and good cooking were not limited to Sundays after church. Both sets of my grandparents loved to cook, and I couldn't wait to go to the markets on Saturday morning with my maternal grandfather. We started early, taking the bus to various neighborhoods where we collected ingredients such as smoked fish and meat, cheeses, and pickles. The smells in those stores intoxicated me. After we had gathered everything on our list we returned home for a lunch of soup and a spread of these wonderful things.

Looking back on my childhood, I realize that my family always ate according to the seasons. We never bought tomatoes from a store because we only ate them after they had ripened on the vines in the backyard. We saved the seasons by pickling and preserving. In the winter we ate hearty soups and stews that had been simmering on the stove most of the day. Spring was focused on Easter, the only time we ate kulich and pashka. Eating well was the way we showed our love for each other. I may have been impatient in church, but even as a child I sensed that there was something spiritual about gathering together over a carefully prepared meal.

It has taken me a while to realize how all of these childhood experiences have influenced who I am and how I cook today. I didn't start out thinking I'd make a career in food. I actually wanted to be a great painter. I even went to art school before realizing that I didn't have much talent in this line nor did I even like it that much. Realizing that made me understand something else: if you want to be good at something you have to love what you do. I love good food, so why not do something with that? Maybe there was a niche for me in the food world.

My career in food has taken me from selling sandwiches in San Francisco offices, to private catering, to opening a restaurant, Lora, in New York, to my present job as food editor of *House & Garden* magazine. Still my favorite times are spent cooking for family and friends, and my best memories come from these experiences too.

I have often asked myself if the world really needs another cookbook. I can only answer that by saying that there is only one me and I have been lucky enough to have some truly great meals and some great experiences with food, and I'd like to pass these on. Just as my childhood was enriched by the spiritual dimension of meals with loved ones, my life now takes its meaning from what I offer to the people I love when we get together. It is this communion of food that I want to convey.

By great meals I don't mean fancy or complicated or exotic. Not at all. My style of cooking involves simple straightforward preparation using the very best seasonal ingredients. I am part of a movement of people who believe in the possiblity of better food and better life through supporting local farmers who grow organically. Alice Waters has been our inspiration and there are enough of us now to make a difference. The strength of our belief can be seen in the huge growth in farmer's markets and in the many different ways we approach food. Each of us takes our beliefs in a new direction. This book is my small contribution to the future of food and community in this country.

In nearly every chapter of this book I will stress the importance of buying seasonally and eating locally. It may seem like a difficult feat, but soon you will learn to take advantage of whatever is freshest.

I do sometimes include luxurious ingredients like truffles (when I can get good ones at the height of their season) for special occasions, and I sometimes suggest a special piece of equipment such as a copper tart tatin pan. A luxurious ingredient is not there to impress your guests; I approach it as I approach asparagus—something beautiful that we are lucky to have once in a while. As for the tart tatin pan, I know it is important to the success of the tart; I have made hundreds of them, so the investment for me is a sound one. Besides the pan is a beautiful object.

When I was a child dreaming of how my lunch would look on its plate, when I was a student cooking for other art students, and now as I prepare a meal for friends, I have always wanted a meal to be beautiful—not fancy, not arranged to resemble a building or a flower, just beautiful the way food is all by itself. When I began thinking about this book, I knew I wanted to work with someone who understood my cooking and my point of view. I thought at once of my friend Tessa Traeger. Her photographs capture what I mean in a way that words can't. Where I am earthy, she is sublime. She makes you see the essence of a fruit or vegetable; she captures its spirit. My hope is that these menus do the very same thing.

Spring Menus

Summer Menus

Autumn Menus

Winter Menus

SPRING

Spring, worth waiting for...

ASPARAGUS WITH EGGS, PARMIGIANO, AND SHALLOT VINAIGRETTE
FILLET OF SALMON COOKED ON A BED OF SALT AND AROMATIC SPICES
COUSCOUS WITH FRESH MORELS AND FAVA BEANS
RHUBARB CRISP

We are so used to seeing certain ingredients in our markets all year round that we scarcely give them a thought. Asparagus and salmon are good examples of foods that are always available, and yet neither tastes the way it should except in season. Wild salmon is so different from the farm-raised variety that I don't often eat this fish unless I can get it at its peak. (When I was growing up in San Francisco we didn't see salmon in our local grocery store until spring because that is when it is caught locally.) Spring is still the time when I look forward to having it. The same is true for asparagus, which, at its best, does not resemble the perfectly cylindrical spears we usually see but is long and thin, a little raggedy, and perfectly tender and sweet.

At my restaurant, salmon was always the most popular entrée. It is still my favorite fish, especially early in its season, from April to late May, when it is at its most delicate. As spring moves into summer, salmon matures and gets oilier so the flesh is often too firm for a simple preparation like the one below. Mature salmon is better suited to a heartier preparation, for instance one with a sauce of garlic and tomatoes.

ASPARAGUS WITH EGGS, PARMIGIANO, AND SHALLOT VINAIGRETTE

SERVES 4

ASPARAGUS

1 pound thin asparagus

1 tablespoon olive oil

1 teaspoon sea salt, plus more for sprinkling

1 hard-boiled egg, chopped

½ cup shaved Parmigiano

2 tablespoons chopped fresh parsley

Freshly ground black pepper to taste

SHALLOT VINAIGRETTE

1 shallot, peeled and finely minced (approximately 2 tablespoons)

2 tablespoons sherry vinegar

1 tablespoon red wine vinegar

6 tablespoons extra-virgin olive oil

¾ teaspoon sea salt

Freshly ground black pepper to taste

There are many different ways to enjoy asparagus in season. The combination of these ingredients is not only delicious but the way they are layered makes a gorgeous presentation. For me this dish is often a meal in itself.

Preheat the oven to 400 degrees.

PREPARE THE ASPARAGUS: If thin asparagus are not available, peel the bottom half of each asparagus with a vegetable peeler and trim one inch off the end of each stalk. Place the asparagus in a nonreactive baking dish with enough water to barely cover them. Drizzle the olive oil over the asparagus and season with the 1 teaspoon sea salt. Cover tightly with aluminum foil or a lid and bake for 20 minutes or until tender when pierced with a sharp knife.

MEANWHILE, PREPARE THE SHALLOT VINAIGRETTE: Mix the shallots and vinegars in a small bowl. Let the mixture sit for 15 minutes. Slowly whisk in the extra-virgin olive oil, and then the salt and pepper to taste.

Remove the pan from the oven, take the asparagus out of the water and place them on a large serving platter or divide them among 4 individual plates. Sprinkle the chopped egg over the asparagus, then drizzle the shallot vinaigrette over the eggs and asparagus. Sprinkle with the Parmigiano, parsley, sea salt, and pepper. Serve slightly warm.

FILLET OF SALMON COOKED ON A BED OF SALT AND AROMATIC SPICES

SERVES 4

2 cups kosher salt

2 3-inch pieces cinnamon, crushed

4 star anise

8 whole cloves

1 teaspoon peppercorns

4 6-ounce salmon fillets

Requires 1 hour advance preparation

The only reservation I have about cooking salmon is that the smell lingers in my apartment for days—no incense or scented candle can get rid of it. I recently discovered that cooking fish on a bed of salt infused with some wonderful aromatic spices significantly reduces the smell and the aromatic spices delicately permeate the salmon.

Preheat the oven to 375 degrees.

In a mixing bowl, combine the kosher salt, cinnamon, star anise, cloves, and peppercorns and toss. Spread the spice mixture evenly over the bottom of a heavy-duty earthenware or enameled baking dish. Lay the salmon fillets, skin side down, on the mixture allowing one inch between each fillet. Cut out a piece of parchment paper to fit inside the dish and place it over the salmon. Cover the dish tightly with aluminum foil.

Place the dish in the preheated oven and bake for 20 minutes for medium, or, if you prefer the salmon well done, continue baking for an additional 5 minutes. Remove the salmon from the oven and allow the fish to rest for 3 minutes. Remove the foil and parchment. Using a long metal spatula, place each fillet on an individual bed of the couscous, leaving its skin behind.

COUSCOUS WITH FRESH MORELS AND FAVA BEANS

If you are not able to find fresh morels, substitute shiitake mushrooms. I found this method for cooking couscous in Claudia Roden's book, THE NEW BOOK OF MIDDLE EASTERN FOOD. The technique is flawless.

Preheat the oven to 400 degrees.

Place the couscous in a lightly oiled ovenproof ceramic baking dish approximately 8 inches by 10 inches. Dissolve the salt in the boiling water. Slowly pour the boiling water over the couscous, stirring well until all the water is absorbed. Using a kitchen fork, continue fluffing the couscous to avoid lumping. Let the couscous rest for 5 minutes and then stir in 1 tablespoon of the olive oil. Place the couscous uncovered in the oven and bake for 10 minutes. Remove and fluff again with the fork. Set aside.

Bring a large pot of salted water to a boil. Prepare an ice bath (a bowl of water and ice with which to shock the fava beans after they have been blanched). Add the fava beans to the boiling water and cook for 1 minute. Drain the beans in a colander and immediately place them in the ice bath for 5 minutes. Drain the cooled beans in the colander. Discard the skins of the beans and set the beans aside.

Melt the butter and remaining 1 tablespoon olive oil in a 12-inch skillet over medium-high heat. Add the morels and shallots, raise the heat to high, and sauté the vegetables for 2 minutes, stirring frequently. Add the fava beans and cook for 30 seconds more. Add the couscous and mix well. When the couscous is heated thoroughly, turn off the heat. Season with sea salt and pepper to taste and serve.

SERVES 4

1 cup couscous

$\frac{1}{2}$ teaspoon sea salt, plus more for sprinkling

1 cup boiling water

2 tablespoons olive oil

1 cup fava beans removed from the pods but skin still on

2 tablespoons unsalted butter

$\frac{1}{4}$ pound fresh morels, cut in half or quartered depending on their size and brushed clean

2 shallots, finely minced (approximately 3 tablespoons)

Freshly ground black pepper

SERVES 6 TO 8

*1 teaspoon unsalted butter,
room temperature*

TOPPING

½ cup raw almonds
¾ cup unbleached all-purpose flour
½ teaspoon sea salt
¼ teaspoon ground allspice
¼ teaspoon cinnamon
¼ cup steel-cut oats
¼ cup packed light brown sugar
*6 tablespoons cold unsalted butter cut
into ¼ -inch pieces*

FILLING

1½ pounds rhubarb
1 cup granulated sugar
*Finely grated zest and juice of one orange
(about 1 tablespoon zest, ½ cup juice)*
1 teaspoon grated fresh ginger

Requires 1 hour advance preparation

It is a staple of food folklore that eating rhubarb in the spring will clean out your system after a winter of heavy foods. True or not, I do feel there is something bracing about the taste of the first rhubarb that appears in the market. Depending on where you live, rhubarb can be found as early as May and then reappear again as late as September.

In making crisps, I vary my toppings according to the fruit used. A peach crisp merits a light topping, but for rhubarb, I want something more substantial like the fruit itself. And I'd certainly serve this dessert with a little freshly whipped cream or a vanilla ice cream.

Preheat the oven to 350 degrees. Grease a 14-by-9-inch baking dish with a teaspoon of butter.

MAKE THE TOPPING: Place the almonds on a baking sheet and bake for 10 minutes or until lightly golden. Remove from the oven and cool. Finely grind ¼ cup of the almonds and roughly chop the rest. Mix together and reserve.

Sift together the flour, salt, allspice, and cinnamon. Add the oats, brown sugar, and all the almonds. Using your fingers, work the butter into the flour mixture, until the mixture forms pea-size pieces and almost comes together but is still crumbly. Reserve.

PREPARE THE FILLING: Cut both ends off the rhubarb and remove the leaves. Using a vegetable peeler, peel the stalks and then slice into ½-inch pieces. In a mixing bowl, toss the rhubarb with the sugar, orange zest and juice, and the ginger.

Spoon the filling into the prepared baking dish, and sprinkle the crisp topping over it. Bake in the preheated oven for 45 minutes or until the topping is golden brown. Remove from the oven and let rest for 5 minutes. Serve warm.

A late breakfast not brunch

TORTINA DI CARCIOFI: OPEN-FACED ARTICHOKE OMELET

FRISÉE SALAD WITH WARM BACON VINAIGRETTE

TOASTED PITA WITH SALTED SWEET BUTTER

CHERRY CLAFOUTIS

I have a problem with the word brunch—an ugly word made up of two perfectly good ones. Let's call that noontime omelet late breakfast, and let's enjoy the luxury of eating our first meal as far into the day as we like. I like the romance of that.

Now that we have established that it's okay to eat eggs after noon and still call it breakfast, here is my twist on the most famous breakfast ingredients—eggs and bacon.

Makes one 9-inch omelet

This recipe for Tortino di Carciofi comes from one of my favorite trattorias in Florence, Sostanza. A Tortino di Carciofi is similar to a frittata (rather than an omelet) in which you add fried artichokes to beaten eggs.

SERVES 2 TO 3

2 baby artichokes (about 6 ounces total)

Juice from 1 lemon

¼ cup all-purpose flour

½ cup extra-virgin olive oil, plus 3 tablespoons

1 teaspoon plus 1 pinch sea salt

6 large fresh eggs, at room temperature

Remove the outer leaves of the artichoke until you get to the inner pale-green tender ones. You will remove about half the leaves. Cut 1½ inches off the top of each artichoke, then cut all but ½ inch off each stem. Cut each artichoke lengthwise into 4 even slices.

Put the artichoke slices in a bowl and cover with cold water and the lemon juice. After 5 minutes, drain them in a colander and shake off any excess water. Pat the slices dry on paper towels and place them in a bowl with the flour. Toss to coat. Place a skillet over medium-high heat and add ¼ cup of the olive oil and the artichokes. Fry them over medium-low heat on both sides until golden brown, about 4 minutes on each side, then remove them from the pan, sprinkle with the 1 teaspoon salt and reserve.

In a small mixing bowl, beat the eggs with a pinch of salt for 1 minute. Heat 3 tablespoons of extra-virgin olive oil in a 9-inch straight sided cast-iron skillet until very hot.

Add the artichoke slices, then add the eggs and, holding the handle firmly in front of you with both hands, begin making small rapid circles in a clockwise motion so the omelet spins around and around in the pan while the bottom of the pan is always touching the burner. The eggs should be moist but not runny.

Do not turn it upside down! Slide the omelet onto a plate. If there is too much excess oil on the plate, transfer the omelet to another plate.

Trattoria SOSTANZA

FIRENZE - Via Porcellana, 25 r

Lista del 11/01/01

Tortino di carciofi

Preparazione

comprare i carciofi, i migliori di stagione
togliere le foglie esterne, tutte le più verdi
fino ad arrivare alle più bianche interne
Tagliare la cima del carciofo fino a circa metà (le punte)
Tagliare a fette per lungo (spessore 1 cm, 2-3 fette)
Tagliare il gambo che ne rimanga solo 2-3 cm
e pulirlo della parte esterna.
Mettere le fette in un recipiente con acqua e limone
spremuto, togliere dall'acqua, infarinarle, metterle
in una padella con olio caldo*, non troppo caldo,
salarle leggermente, rosolarle da ambo le parti
e metterli da parte.
Mettere l'olio nel tegamino, quando è ben caldo
ci si mettono 3 o 4 fette di carciofo
sbattere l'uovo nella scodilla, salare leggermente
e metterlo contemporaneamente nel tegame
dei carciofi e GIRARLO ⟳ per
amalgamare l'uovo - senza capovolgerlo!
                    Buon Affetito!
P.S. Se c'è troppo olio nel piatto cambiare il
piatto

* la Sostanza i fornelli
sono a carbone e l'olio
sempre extra-vergine

FRISÉE SALAD WITH WARM BACON VINAIGRETTE

SERVES 4

1 head frisée lettuce (about ½ pound)
3 tablespoons red wine vinegar
3 tablespoons extra-virgin olive oil
1 shallot, finely minced
1 clove garlic, finely minced
½ pound bacon, cut into 1-by-¼-inch lardons
1 tablespoon chopped fresh parsley
Sea salt and freshly ground black pepper to taste

This salad is my version of a classic *frisée au lardons*, which is often served with a poached egg. For the best results the frisée must be very cold and dry and the salad must be served immediately after adding the vinaigrette. Wrapping the frisée in paper towels instead of tea towels allows the frisée to cool and dry more quickly, and leaves just enough moisture to crisp it perfectly.

Wash and dry the frisée, and wrap in paper towels. Refrigerate until ready to serve. In a small bowl combine the red wine vinegar, olive oil, shallot, and garlic.

Sauté the bacon lardons in a skillet over medium-high heat until golden brown and crisp. Transfer the bacon to a plate lined with paper towels and pat dry. Reserve. Discard all but 1 tablespoon of the bacon fat from the skillet. (Be careful of the hot oil.)

Remove the frisée from the refrigerator, and place it in a large bowl. Place the pan with the reserved bacon fat back on the heat. When warm, add the vinaigrette. Turn off the heat and whisk the dressing. Pour it over the frisée. Add the bacon lardons and parsley and toss. Season with salt and pepper and serve immediately.

TOASTED PITA WITH SALTED SWEET BUTTER

SERVES 4

5 tablespoons unsalted butter
2 whole pita breads, sliced in half to make 2 disks each
Fleur de sel to taste or any good-quality salt

Whenever I want salted butter, I add salt to European sweet butter rather than buying domestic salted butter. There are several reasons for this. Most salt in commercial butter is there as a preservative. The shelf life of sweet butter is much shorter, making it more likely to be fresh. Secondly, when you buy European sweet butter it has a higher fat content, and tastes much richer. Then, if you want salted butter you can control it by adding the desired amount of salt. Fleur de sel, which means the flower of sea, is a delicate, high-quality salt harvested from the sea. It is my favorite salt to use with butter.

Preheat the broiler.

Melt the butter in a small saucepan over low heat. Place the pita halves, cut side up, on a baking sheet and brush the tops with the melted butter. Toast in the broiler until the pita is lightly browned.

Place the toasted pita on a chopping board; slice each half into 3 triangles, season with some fleur de sel and serve warm.

CHERRY CLAFOUTIS

This clafoutis is a chic breakfast dessert. Prepare it as close to serving time as you can, so the cherries are still a little warm. I leave the pits in the cherries because the fruit holds its shape better and the juice does not escape. However, for ease of eating you can certainly pit them. If you don't, be sure to let your guests know beforehand.

Using an earthenware baking dish (see Sources) for this recipe gives the best results because the whole dish heats at the same time and therefore cooks evenly.

Preheat the oven to 400 degrees.

Place the cherries in an earthenware baking dish just large enough for the cherries to all lay flat. Sprinkle them with the sugar. Bake for 15 minutes. Remove the pan from the oven and gently place the cherries in a strainer for 15 minutes to drain off any excess liquid. Discard the liquid.

Reduce the oven temperature to 350 degrees. Wash and dry the same baking dish and then coat it with the butter.

Beat the eggs and sugar together until light and fluffy, about 2 minutes. Mix in the crème fraîche, heavy cream, and reserved vanilla bean seeds. Stir in the flour. Let this batter rest for 15 minutes.

Place the cherries back in the buttered earthenware dish in one layer. Pour the batter over the cherries and bake for 35 minutes or until the top is firm and golden brown. Remove the clafoutis from the oven and let rest for 10 minutes. Dust with confectioners' sugar and serve.

SERVES 6

1 pound firm fresh cherries, washed and stems removed

1 tablespoon sugar

1 teaspoon unsalted butter

3 eggs, at room temperature

1/2 cup sugar

1/2 cup crème fraîche

1/4 cup heavy cream

1 vanilla bean, cut in half, seeds scraped out and reserved

1/2 cup unbleached all-purpose flour

Confectioners' sugar, for dusting

It's all about green

LORA'S GUACAMOLE

ENGLISH PEA SOUP WITH CRÈME FRAÎCHE

RISOTTO VERDE

BASIL ICE CREAM WITH LEMON CLOVE COOKIES

Just as the colors of nature change to reflect the seasons, so do the colors of the foods we've come to associate with them. In summer tomatoes are a vibrant red, and corn is available in gorgeous shades of yellow. In autumn we enjoy the orange hues of squashes and pumpkins, and in winter the cool steel color of oysters. But no seasonal color is as striking to me as the green found in the foods of spring, and no tastes and textures are as welcome as those of spring vegetables. To have a spring onion mild enough to be eaten raw with just a little salt, or perfectly tender beans, or sweet peas just picked from the vine are treasured experiences.

I had never given much thought to the connection between the seasons and colors of my ingredients until I first went to Ireland. As I looked down from the airplane, I could not believe that there were so many different shades of green in nature. Since then, spring has taken on new meaning for me and it is about the pleasures of that color—about asparagus, peas, fava beans, spring onions.

Here is a simple collection of my favorite green recipes inspired by that trip to Ireland.

LORA'S GUACAMOLE

Requires 1½ hours advance preparation

MAKES 2 ½ CUPS

3 ripe avocados

Freshly squeezed juice of 2 limes

¼ cup minced spring onion or scallions

¼ cup fresh cilantro leaves, washed, dried well, and minced

1 jalapeño chile, minced (about 1 tablespoon)

1 tablespoon extra-virgin olive oil

1½ teaspoons sea salt

Freshly ground black pepper to taste

While making guacamole one afternoon, I realized that almost all the ingredients I used were green. Maybe it's because tomatoes were not in season or because I like the sharp bite of limes rather than lemons or because I love young spring onions instead of yellow. I am not sure, but the result speaks for itself. When you work with chile peppers, be careful not to rub your eyes because the oil from the chiles gets on your hands and can burn your eyes.

Cut the avocados in half vertically. Discard the pit and slice each half in half. Remove the peels, and place the avocado pieces in a mixing bowl. Add the lime juice. With a potato masher or kitchen fork, mash the avocados. Add the onion, cilantro, jalapeño, olive oil, salt, and pepper, and mix. Transfer the guacamole to a serving bowl. Cover and refrigerate for 1 hour before serving.

ENGLISH PEA SOUP WITH CRÈME FRAÎCHE

SERVES 4

3 pounds fresh English peas, shelled (about 3¾ cups)

2 tablespoons unsalted butter

1 small onion, finely chopped (about 1 cup)

1 carrot, peeled and cut into ¼-inch dice

1 quart water

2 teaspoons sea salt, plus more to taste

Freshly ground black pepper

¼ cup crème fraîche

As a child I detested peas. I would sit for what seemed like hours after everyone had left the dinner table until I ate my peas. Then as an adult I bought some fresh English peas in the spring at the farmer's market and my love affair began. Since they are my new best friend, here is a soup I just can't get enough of in the height of the season.

The key to this soup is to make it as soon as possible after buying your peas. The sugar-to-starch conversion process begins as soon as the peas are picked so the fresher, the better. It is also important to chill the peas before and after cooking. This helps them retain their vibrant color.

Place the peas in a large bowl of ice water.

In a 4-quart saucepan, melt the butter over medium-high heat. Add the onion and carrot and cook over medium-low heat until the vegetables are wilted and the onions are transparent, about 5 minutes. Add the water and salt and bring to a boil.

Fill a large bowl half-way with ice water and place a slightly smaller bowl in it. You will use this to chill the soup immediately after it has cooked.

When the water is boiling, remove the peas from the ice water, add them to the soup, and cook for 1 minute. Immediately pour the soup into the bowl set into the ice bath. Stir until cool.

When the soup is completely cool, place it in a blender and puree until smooth. Pour the soup back into the saucepan, heat to simmer and add salt and pepper to taste. Pour into individual soup bowls. Place 1 tablespoon of crème fraîche in the center of each bowl and serve immediately.

RISOTTO VERDE

On my first visit to Rome, I stumbled across a small trattoria near Campo De Fiori whose kitchen emitted wonderful aromas—a sure sign that the food would be delicious. I ordered a risotto verde, never having had one before and out came a mound of rice in a mélange of beautiful green shades. At home I immediately tried to re-create what I had eaten in Rome.

Even rice has a shelf life. Buy quality rice for risotto—I prefer Italian Arborio or Canaroli—with an expiration date on the bag or box. Always store rice in a cool dark location in an airtight container.

Soak the spinach and arugula leaves separately in water for 30 minutes to remove all the grit and sand.

Heat a 10- to 12-inch skillet and add the washed spinach leaves. Sauté for several minutes, stirring, until wilted. Place the spinach in a colander and drain well, then finely chop.

Drain the arugula leaves and roughly chop. Wash and drain the parsley leaves and roughly chop.

Place the stock in a saucepan and bring to a boil. Reduce the heat to a high simmer. Skim off any scum that rises to the surface.

In a 6-quart nonreactive saucepan, melt the olive oil and butter. Add the shallots and garlic and stir over low heat for 2 minutes. Add the rice and continue stirring for another minute or until the rice is translucent. Add the white wine and cook over medium heat until all the liquid has been absorbed. Add 1 teaspoon salt. Then using a ladle, begin adding the warm stock approximately 1 cup at a time, stirring with a wooden spoon several times after each addition. Wait until the stock has been absorbed before adding more. Repeat this until almost all the stock has been absorbed and the rice is al dente. The cooking time for the risotto is approximately 35 minutes.

Stir in the chopped spinach, chopped arugula, chopped parsley, and peas. Cook for 4 minutes, stirring occasionally. Remove from the heat and stir in the heavy cream and 1/2 cup of the Parmigiano. Season with the red pepper and add salt and black pepper. Serve immediately, passing the remaining Parmigiano separately.

SERVES 4

6 cups spinach leaves firmly packed with stems removed

3 cups arugula leaves firmly packed

1 cup lightly packed flat-leaf parsley leaves (about 1/2 ounce)

4 1/2 cups chicken or vegetable stock

3 tablespoons extra-virgin olive oil

1 tablespoon unsalted butter

2 shallots, finely minced (about 1/4 cup)

1 clove garlic, peeled and crushed

1 1/4 cups Arborio rice (see Sources)

1 cup dry white wine

1 teaspoon sea salt, plus more for seasoning

1/2 cup fresh shelled peas, chilled in ice water

1/4 cup heavy cream

1 cup grated Parmigiano

1/2 teaspoon freshly ground red pepper (optional)

Freshly ground black pepper to taste

BASIL ICE CREAM

Requires 3 hours advance preparation

MAKES 1 QUART

2 cups heavy cream

2 cups whole milk

1 teaspoon vanilla extract

7 egg yolks

1/2 cup sugar

1 cup tightly packed basil leaves, washed

Fill a large bowl with ice water and place another bowl in it, large enough to hold the cream mixture. Have a mesh sieve ready.

Combine the cream, milk, and vanilla extract in a 2-quart saucepan over medium-high heat until warm, about 125 degrees.

Whisk the egg yolks together, then add the sugar and whisk until a ribbon forms, about 1 minute.

Slowly pour a little warm cream into the egg mixture, whisking as you pour. Gradually pour in the rest of the cream, stirring constantly. Once you have added all the cream, pour the mixture into the saucepan and bring it to a medium-high simmer, stirring continuously until the mixture thickens and coats the back of a spoon or is 170 degrees, about 10 to 12 minutes. Remove from the heat and immediately pour the cream through the sieve into the large bowl in the ice bath. Stir the mixture for several minutes to speed the cooling.

When the mixture is cool, add all the basil. In a food processor or blender, puree the mixture until it is green, about 30 seconds. You can do this in two batches if necessary. Refrigerate the ice cream base for at least 2 hours before freezing. Freeze in an ice-cream machine according to the manufacturer's instructions.

LEMON CLOVE COOKIES

Requires 3 hours advance preparation

MAKES 3 DOZEN

DOUGH

1 3/4 cups unbleached all-purpose flour

1/4 teaspoon ground cloves

1/4 teaspoon salt

1/4 cup blanched almonds, finely ground

2 sticks (1/2 pound) unsalted butter, cut into 1-inch cubes, at room temperature

3/4 cup sugar

1 egg yolk

Finely grated zest from 1 lemon, organic

TOPPING

3 tablespoons sugar

1/8 teaspoon ground cloves

MAKE THE DOUGH: Sift the flour, cloves, and salt into a mixing bowl. Stir in the ground almonds.

Using an electric mixer, beat together the butter and sugar until light and fluffy, about 2 minutes Beat in the egg yolk and lemon zest and then gradually add the flour mixture until well incorporated. The dough should be crumbly but hold together.

Place the dough on a lightly floured work surface. Using your hands, roll into a log, approximately 2 inches in diameter. Wrap the log in plastic wrap and refrigerate for at least 3 hours.

Preheat the oven to 350 degrees.

MAKE THE TOPPING: Combine the 3 tablespoons sugar and ground cloves and reserve.

Line two baking sheets with parchment paper. Remove the dough from the refrigerator and place it on a cutting board. Slice the dough into 1/4-inch slices. Place the cookies 1 inch apart on the baking sheets.

Bake for 12 to 15 minutes or until the edges are a light, golden brown. Remove from the oven and sprinkle with the sugar-clove topping.

Lunch with the Humbrechts

WHITE ASPARAGUS WITH FROMAGE BLANC AIOLI, SERVED WITH SMOKED HAMS

1990 DOMAINE ZIND HUMBRECHT, MUSCAT

MUENSTER CHEESES

1990 DOMAINE ZIND HUMBRECHT, GEWÜRZTRAMINER, CLOS WINDSBUHL

OLIVIER'S GRANDMOTHER'S WALNUT CAKE

1990 DOMAINE ZIND HUMBRECHT, RIESLING, BRAND VT

Several of my most memorable food experiences have come during my travels in France. One in particular involved a visit with the great winemaker, Olivier Humbrecht, in Alsace. On a spectacular spring morning I met Olivier at his winery for a tasting, and then went on to have lunch with him, his wife, Margaret, and some of their friends from London.

That lunch was the essence of what I love most in a meal: simplicity, quality, and seasonality. Margaret served large platters of organic white asparagus fresh from the farmer's market with a wonderful fromage blanc aioli, a platter of smoked ham, delicious raw milk Muenster cheese, and a simple walnut cake with strawberries. I think everyone had at least three helpings of everything.

And the wines were a revelation. Like most Americans I was largely ignorant of the great range of Alsatian wines, nor did I realize that they improve with age. Olivier himself produces more than 35 wines from vineyards all over Alsace. In some vineyards he may own only two of the rows or so, in others he may own the whole vineyard. Wherever his wines come from, he has paid close attention to every detail of soil and environment.

I left entirely happy, as did the other guests, especially the couple from London who loaded their car with enough Zind Humbrecht wines to last them until the next spring. By the time these two had finished packing the car, it was clear that there was only enough room for the driver so the wife stayed on and made arrangements for a flight home. I eventually learned that this was their annual ritual that got them happily from one year to the next.

WHITE ASPARAGUS WITH FROMAGE BLANC AIOLI,
SERVED WITH SMOKED HAMS

SERVES 4 TO 6

3 pounds fresh white asparagus
Sea salt to taste
½ pound smoked speck ham, thinly sliced
½ pound smoked ham, thinly sliced
1 cup Fromage Blanc Aioli (recipe follows)

White asparagus is not as common an ingredient in America as it is in France in the spring. They are, however, seen for a fleeting moment in American farmers markets; if you can't find them there, imported white asparagus is available in specialty grocery stores.

Peel the asparagus with a vegetable peeler. Cut one inch off the bottom of each stalk. Tie the asparagus into 2 equal bundles using kitchen string. Bring a large pot of salted water to a boil. Add the asparagus, bring the water back to the boil, and cook for 10 minutes or until tender. Use kitchen tongs to remove the asparagus bundles from the water and place them in a colander to drain. Transfer the bundles onto a platter, remove the string, and sprinkle the asparagus with sea salt. Serve warm along with the ham and fromage blanc aioli.

FROMAGE BLANC AIOLI

Margaret serves a fromage blanc aioli along with a bowl of classic aioli, a garlic mayonnaise, as it is lighter and less rich for those who are watching their weight. These garlicky sauces are ideal accompaniments to the asparagus and ham.

MAKES 1 CUP

1 cup fromage blanc

¼ cup Garlic Aioli (see page 101)

1 tablespoon Dijon mustard

2 tablespoons chopped chives

Sea salt and freshly ground pepper to taste

Combine all the ingredients in a bowl and mix well. Cover and refrigerate for at least 2 hours before serving.

OLIVIER'S GRANDMOTHER'S WALNUT CAKE

Requires 1 hour advance preparation

When it came time for dessert, I did not think I could eat one more thing. But this cake was very light and wonderful with the dessert wine. Olivier poured a 1990 Riesling, Brand Vineyard VT with the cake. VT simply means *Vendages Tardives*, late harvest. The grapes are picked at their optimum ripeness, which produces a rich sauternes-like wine. The walnutty cake went well with the concentrated flavors of lychee and apricots in the wine.

SERVES 6 TO 8

1 stick (4 ounces) unsalted butter, at room temperature

3 cups shelled walnut halves (about 11 ounces)

1 cup sugar

5 eggs, at room temperature

½ cup all-purpose flour

2 tablespoons kirsch

Confectioners' sugar, for dusting

Preheat the oven to 350 degrees.

Use 2 teaspoons of the butter to grease the inside of a 9-inch round cake pan. Cut a piece of parchment paper to fit the bottom of the pan and press it in. Butter the paper with 1 teaspoon of the butter.

Place the walnuts on a baking sheet and bake for 10 minutes or until they darken slightly. Remove them from the oven and cool. Use a food processor to grind the walnuts to a fine powder, set aside.

Beat the remaining butter with the sugar in a mixing bowl until light and fluffy, about 2 minutes. Beat in the eggs one at a time. Then add the ground nuts, flour, and kirsch, and mix well. Pour the mixture into the prepared pan and bake for 30 minutes or until a cake tester inserted in the center of the cake comes out dry. Remove the cake from the oven. When cool, remove from the cake pan. Discard the parchment paper and dust the top of the cake with confectioners' sugar.

A Russian Easter on Potrero Hill

GRILLED SHASHLIK

RICE PILAF WITH ALMONDS

CREMINI MUSHROOMS AND BABY ONIONS IN SOUR CREAM AND DILL

AUNT NINA'S KULICH AND PASKHA

As a child, Easter was always my favorite holiday—except for the Easter outfit with its uncomfortable shoes and a hat that made me feel ridiculous. I couldn't wait to get home from church, throw off the clothes, and eat.

Whenever my large Russian family gathered for a special occasion, food was at the center of it, with both my grandmothers cooking for days beforehand to make a bountiful spread. Russians love to eat and we love to have a buffet with lots and lots of choices. No one ever left either of my grandmothers' tables hungry.

At Easter, we dyed eggs the night before like other kids, but there was another fascinating ritual going on at the same time. My favorite grandmother was making kulich—an Easter bread that is served with paskha, a cheese spread—on Easter morning. The bread is set to rise the evening before, punched down throughout the night, and then baked in the morning. I never really understood why you couldn't make it the day before, but you just didn't. My grandmother told me that one year she was so tired she actually slept with her kulich so she could punch it down without having to get up and go to the kitchen. I feel very lucky to have these memories.

A complete Russian Easter menu would fill a book, so here are just a few of my favorite dishes, including the famous Kulich with Paskha.

GRILLED SHASHLIK

Requires 24 hours advance preparation

Every year my father and his brothers took turns making shashlik, a Russian lamb kebab dish in which the lamb is marinated for 24 hours and then grilled. There was always an argument as to whose was better. One added wine, one didn't, and one used only lemon juice. Of course I always thought my father's was the best. This recipe is inspired by his.

Trim off any excess fat from the lamb and cut the meat into 2-by-2-inch cubes. Place the lamb in a nonreactive bowl. Stir in all the remaining ingredients and marinate, covered, for 24 hours in the refrigerator. Stir the meat several times while it marinates.

Remove the lamb from the refrigerator one hour before grilling. Start your coals in your grill and prepare a very hot fire. Remove the lamb from the marinating liquid and drain in a colander. When your fire is ready, place the pieces of lamb on the grill. (It is important that the pieces of lamb are grilled separately and not on a skewer. This makes them cook evenly and quickly.) Grill the lamb approximately 3 to 4 minutes on each side for medium rare or 5 to 6 minutes for medium well. When the lamb is cooked, remove from the grill and place on a serving platter. Season with salt and pepper. Serve immediately.

SERVES 6 TO 8

1 butterflied leg of lamb (3½ to 4 pounds)
8 cloves garlic, peeled and thinly sliced
1 medium onion, peeled and grated
⅓ cup extra-virgin olive oil
2 cups dry white wine
Freshly squeezed juice from 3 lemons
Zest from 1 lemon
1 tablespoon sea salt, plus more for seasoning
Freshly ground black pepper

RICE PILAF WITH ALMONDS

Melt the olive oil in a 2-quart saucepan. Add the shallot, almonds, and turmeric, and sauté for 2 minutes. Add the chicken stock or broth and bring to a boil, then add the rice, orzo, and salt. Cover, reduce the heat, and simmer for 20 minutes. Turn off the heat and let sit for 5 minutes before serving.

SERVES 6 TO 8

2 teaspoons olive oil
1 shallot, finely minced (about 3 tablespoons)
¼ cup slivered almonds
⅛ teaspoon turmeric
2¼ cups chicken stock or broth
¾ cups basmati rice
¼ cup orzo
1 teaspoon sea salt

CREMINI MUSHROOMS AND BABY ONIONS IN SOUR CREAM AND DILL

SERVES 6

1 tablespoon unsalted butter

2 tablespoons olive oil

½ pound pearl onions, peeled
(about 2 cups)

1 cup dry white wine

1 pound small cremini mushrooms,
cleaned and sliced in half

1 cup chicken stock

½ cup sour cream

¼ cup fresh dill, coarsely chopped

Sea salt and freshly ground black pepper
to taste

The combination of the ingredients used in this recipe is very Russian to me. The dill and sour cream make a great sauce for the lamb.

Melt the butter in the olive oil in a 12-inch sauté pan. Add the onions and cook over medium heat for 5 to 7 minutes, stirring occasionally so the onions brown on all sides. Turn the heat to high, add the wine and cook until the wine has almost evaporated, about 10 minutes. Add the mushrooms, chicken stock, and sour cream, and cook for 15 to 20 minutes. Stir in the dill and season with salt and pepper.

AUNT NINA'S KULICH

MAKES 5 1 1/2-POUND LOAVES

Yields approximately 7 pounds of dough

KULICH

1 cup light rum

½ cup golden raisins

¾ cup whole milk

¾ cup half-and-half

½ cup sour cream, room temperature

2 packages yeast (5 teaspoons)

1 tablespoon granulated sugar

8 tablespoons unsalted butter
(one stick), melted

1 cup all purpose flour

½ teaspoon salt

1 egg, beaten

24 tablespoons unsalted butter (3 sticks),
cut into ¼-inch cubes

½ teaspoon salt

1½ cups granulated sugar

¼ teaspoon saffron threads soaked in
2 tablespoons vodka

Requires 6 hours advance preparation

This recipe is from my Aunt Nina. She translated and adopted it from my grandmother.

Traditionally my family saved all sorts of cans throughout the year and at Easter baked many different sized kulichs. I have used 48 ounce cans in this recipe for simplification, but you should feel free to experiment. If you do, be sure to you fill the cans only one third full and adjust the baking times accordingly.

Before you start read the directions carefully. It is imperative to have all the ingredients measured and ready to go beforehand or the timing will not work.

TO MAKE THE KULICH: Bring the rum almost to a boil and add the raisins. Turn off the heat, cover and let soak for 1 hour.

Combine the milk and half-and-half and bring almost to a boil. Turn off the heat. Remove ½ cup of the mixture into a bowl and stir in the sour cream. Set the saucepan and bowl aside but keep warm.

In a separate bowl add the yeast and the sugar. Stir in ½ cup of the warm milk mixture, it should be about 110 degrees. Let stand for 5 minutes. The yeast should begin to bubble.

Melt the 8 tablespoons butter in the remaining ½ cup of the milk mixture. Using an electric mixer, beat in the cup of flour and salt. Add the whole beaten egg. Mix thoroughly until well blended. Stir in the yeast mixture. Cover the bowl with plastc wrap and a kitchen towel and place in a warm spot. Let stand for approximately 30 minutes or until the mixture has doubled in bulk.

In another bowl use an electric mixer to beat the 24 tablespoons cubed butter with the ½ teaspoon of salt until light and fluffy, about 3 minutes. Add the sugar, ½ cup at a time, beating in between to keep batter very light. Add the vodka-saffron mixture, vanilla seeds, vanilla extract, orange and lemon zest, ground nutmeg, and ground cardamom, set aside.

In a separate bowl, using an electric mixer, beat the 11 egg yolks until pale and fluffy, about 2 minutes. Very gradually add 1 cup of sugar and continue beating for 30 seconds until incorporated. Add this egg and sugar mixture to the butter and sugar mixture, ½ cup at a time, beating at slow speed. Then stir in the yeast mixture.

Gradually add the sifted flour alternately with the remaining warm milk and sour cream mixture. Continue mixing until dough comes together and it is no longer sticky. Add more all-purpose flour if necessary. The dough will be soft.

Note: Your mixing bowl may be too small for the volume of batter. You can divide the batter into several bowls before adding the flour. Combine the doughs after the flour has been added.

Drain the golden raisins and knead them into the dough. Knead the dough on a floured surface for 15 minutes.

Butter an 8–quart bowl, preferably ceramic, and place the dough into the bowl. Cover with plastic wrap and a kitchen towel and place in a warm environment for about 2 hours, until the dough has doubled in bulk.

While the dough is rising, prepare the cans. Melt ¼ cup butter. Brush the inside of the cans with melted butter and dust with the breadcrumbs.

Tie four-inch collars around each can with string. Collars can be made from brown paper bags or parchment paper.

Line the bottom of each can with a piece of parchment paper. Preheat the oven to warm.

When the dough is ready, punch it down to expel the air. Cut off a 1½ pound piece (2½ cups) and knead on a floured surface. Form the dough into a ball, gently elongate the ball, and place it carefully into the can. The dough should fill up ⅓ of the can. Repeat with all the cans.

Turn off the oven. Place a rack inside a baking pan and rest the cans on top. Fill the baking pan halfway with boiling water. Close the oven door and allow the dough to rise for an hour until doubled in bulk.

1 vanilla bean, split open and seeds scraped out and set aside

1 teaspoon vanilla extract

Zest of 1 orange

Zest of 1 lemon

1 whole nutmeg, finely grated (1 teaspoon)

¼ teaspoon cardamom seeds, finely ground in a mortar, ½ cup chopped almonds

11 egg yolks

1 cup sugar

4½ cups bread flour, 4½ cups all-purpose flour sifted together

¼ cup unsalted butter, melted

5 (48 ounce) tomato cans, empty and washed well

Unseasoned bread crumbs for dusting

FROSTING

1 cup confectioner's sugar

1 tablespoon egg white

1 teaspoon vanilla

Remove the cans from the oven and preheat to 325 degrees.

Return the cans to the oven and bake for 35–40 minutes. To determine if the bread is baked through, stick a long wooden skewer through the middle. It should come out clean. Bread is done when the temperature registers 190–195 degrees on a candy thermometer.

Remove the cans from the oven and let stand for 10 minutes. Gently remove the bread from the cans and lay on towels. Roll them from time to time while cooling to keep the cylindrical shape.

Let cool completely (about 2 hours).

MAKE THE FROSTING: Mix all the ingredients together until smooth. Spread evenly over the tops of the cooled kulich loaves and allow to drip down the sides.

PASKHA

Requires 24 hours advance preparation

MAKES 2½ POUNDS
1½ cups sugar
¾ cup heavy cream
5 egg yolks
1 vanilla bean
4 sticks (1 pound) unsalted butter, at room temperature
2½ pounds farmer's cheese, or uncreamed cottage cheese (about 5 packed cups)
1 cup sour cream
¼ teaspoon salt

We always made paskha, kulich's classic accompaniment in a wooden truncated pyramid mold with "X B" inscribed on the side. (The letters stand for "Christ is risen" in Russian.) These molds are very difficult to find, so I offer an alternative—a colander or flower pot.

If a farmer's cheese is unavailable, simply take regular cottage cheese and hang it in cheesecloth to remove all liquid.

In the top of a double boiler, stir together the sugar, heavy cream, and egg yolks. Cook over medium heat until the sugar is dissolved and the mixture coats a metal spoon, about 15 minutes. Remove from the heat and let cool.

Split the vanilla bean lengthwise with a sharp knife and scrape out the seeds. Place the vanilla seeds and butter in a bowl and beat until fluffy. Add the cheese, sour cream, and salt, mixing until all the ingredients are well combined. Slowly add the cooled cream mixture.

Cut two 32-inch lengths of cheesecloth and rinse. Line a 2-quart clay flower pot or colander with both pieces of the cheesecloth letting the excess hang over the sides. Spoon the cheese mixture into the cloth.

Fold the excess cheesecloth on top of the cheese. Place the flower pot or colander in a larger pan, elevating it so it can drain; cover the top with plastic wrap and place a plate inside the rim. Place a heavy weight on the plate, such as a large canned food. Refrigerate for 24 hours.

Remove from the refrigerator and remove the weight. Fold back the cheesecloth and invert the cheese onto a serving plate. Serve at room temperature. The paskha can be stored in the refrigerator for up to 3 days. Paskha can be frozen but the consistency may change slightly.

You are where you shop

SOUP AU PISTOU

BUTTER LEAF SALAD WITH ANCHOVY, GARLIC, AND LEMON VINAIGRETTE

TOASTED PAIN LEVAIN WITH WARM CABÉCIOU DE ROCAMADOUR

STRAWBERRIES MACERATED WITH MOSCATO D'ASTI

The last time I visited San Francisco I got up extra early on a Saturday to go to the farmer's market at the Ferry Plaza near the Embarcadero. I wanted to beat the rush, but the rush beat me. There was no parking within four blocks of the market and the lines were already long for bread, cheese, poultry, fish, flowers, and vegetables. Fortunately, this is one place where I don't mind waiting in line, and you could see that many other people, here to spend a good part of their day off, didn't either.

You find this kind of enthusiasm in farmer's markets throughout the country but never in the aisles of your local supermarket, which only shows that there are people all over America who want quality. And the more we support local growers and artisans the more of them there will be. The personal connection with the people who raise the food I buy makes each transaction a particular treat. I crave local specialties like those exceptional tamales you can get in the West Hollywood farmer's market, or the hundreds of varieties of spring flower bulbs available at the Madison, Wisconsin market, or the soaps made from foraged plants at the Berkeley market in California. I look forward to seeing the folks from Marshall's Honey in San Francisco or the men from Knoll's Farm who sell me poultry and eggs at Union Square in New York City. These are people who love what they do.

If you live in New York, as I do, spring is an especially exciting time at the farmer's markets. Winter has been banished and everyone is thrilled to see all the things that have at last reappeared. This menu reflects that excitement and includes foods that fill the daily markets across the country in spring.

SOUP AU PISTOU

Requires 12 hours advance preparation

Soup at the right time and right place is so comforting. On rainy days in late spring and early summer, for instance, I am inspired to make Soup au Pistou. The markets are filled with spring lamb, spring vegetables, and the herbs that make this recipe sing.

One of the great pleasures in life for me is getting a chance to use my French soup spoons. I have been collecting these oversized soup spoons for years in various flea markets in France. If ever there was the proper moment to bring them out, it's with Soup au Pistou—you want to get every ingredient of the soup in one spoonful.

In Richard Olney's book LULU'S PROVENCAL TABLE, Lulu adds a lamb shank to her pistou, which gives this dish a wonderful consistency (it is also good without it). If you are lucky enough to find fresh cranberry or white beans, use them (you'll need 1 pound unshelled, approximately ³/₄ cup). The fresh beans will cook in less time so watch them carefully. For conveniences sake I have written the recipe with the dried variety (see Sources).

MAKE THE SOUP: Wash the dried beans and place them in a bowl. Add cool water to cover by 2 inches. Cover and refrigerate overnight. Remove the beans from the refrigerator, rinse, and place in a 6- to 8-quart pot. Add 2 quarts of the cold water and the bouquet garni. Bring the water to a boil, reduce the heat to a high simmer, and cook, partially covered, for 1¹/₂ hours, or until the beans are tender. Use a wide-mesh skimmer or ladle to transfer the beans to a bowl. Discard the bouquet garni. Add the lamb shank to the bean broth along with the remaining 2 quarts of cold water, the salt, onion, and garlic. Bring the liquid back to a boil and cook partially covered, for 1 hour over medium-high heat. Skim as necessary to remove any scum that rises to the surface.

MAKE THE PISTOU WHILE LAMB IS SIMMERING: In a mortar, pound the garlic, salt, and pepper to taste into a paste. Add the basil leaves and crush them into the paste. Add the olive oil in a thin stream, and keep pounding the paste while incorporating the oil. Cover and let sit for up to 1 hour.

Remove the lamb shank and add the reserved cooked beans and the carrots, potatoes, green beans, zucchini, and tomatoes. Continue cooking, partially covered, at a high simmer for an additional hour. Meanwhile, when the lamb is cool enough to handle, cut the meat off the bone and coarsely chop it. Add the chopped lamb back

SERVES 8

SOUP

³/₄ cup dried beans, such as cranberry, white, borlotto, or soldier

4 quarts cold water

1 bouquet garni made with 1 bay leaf, 2 sprigs thyme, 2 stems parsley, and ¹/₄ teaspoon peppercorns tied in cheesecloth

1 lamb shank (about ³/₄ pound)

1 tablespoon sea salt, plus more for seasonings

1 medium onion, finely diced (about 1 cup)

3 cloves garlic, peeled and halved lengthwise

2 medium carrots, peeled and cut into ¹/₄-inch dice

2 medium potatoes, peeled and cut into ¹/₄-inch dice

¹/₂ pound green beans, both ends trimmed, sliced into ¹/₂-inch lengths

2 medium zucchini, cut into ¹/₄-inch dice

3 canned whole tomatoes, seeded and coarsely chopped (about ¹/₂ cup)

1 cup dried pasta, such as elbow, orecchetti, or cavatappi

Freshly ground black pepper

PISTOU

3 large cloves garlic, peeled

1 teaspoon coarse sea salt

Freshly ground black pepper

2 ounces fresh basil leaves, washed and torn into small pieces

¹/₄ cup extra-virgin olive oil

1 cup grated Parmigiano cheese

to the soup while it is cooking. (The soup can be made in advance up to this point and refrigerated for up to two days.) Bring the soup to a boil and add the pasta. Cook over high heat for 15 minutes or until the pasta is al dente.

Remove the soup from the heat and stir in the pistou. Season with salt and pepper to taste. Pass the grated Parmigiano cheese.

BUTTER LEAF SALAD WITH ANCHOVY, GARLIC, AND LEMON VINAIGRETTE

Requires 1 hour advance preparation

When I serve this salad, everyone loves the vinaigrette, even people who don't like anchovies. Before you serve a good vinaigrette, it's of the utmost importance that your lettuce is very dry and crisp before you dress it. Also, I use a wooden bowl when tossing a salad. This allows the vinaigrette to better adhere to the lettuce.

Pair this salad with the Toasted Pain Levain (recipe follows).

Discard several of the outer leaves of the lettuce. Wash and dry the remaining lettuce leaves, wrap them in paper towels, and refrigerate for at least 1 hour and up to 24 hours before serving.

To make the vinaigrette, mince the anchovies fillets and garlic. Combine them with the salt in a small wooden mixing bowl or mortar and mash into a smooth paste. Whisk in the salt, lemon juice, and red wine vinegar. Then whisk in the olive oil.

To serve, toss the lettuce in a salad bowl with half the vinaigrette. Taste and add more vinaigrette if necessary. Season with freshly ground pepper and more salt if needed.

SERVES 6

2 heads butterhead lettuce (about 1 pound)

4 oil-packed anchovy fillets, drained on paper towels

1 clove garlic, peeled

1 teaspoon coarse sea salt, plus more for seasonings

Freshly squeezed juice of 1 lemon (about 2 tablespoons)

1 tablespoon red wine vinegar

6 tablespoons extra-virgin olive oil

Freshly ground black pepper

TOASTED PAIN LEVAIN WITH WARM CABÉCIOU DE ROCAMADOUR

Pain levain is a hearty French bread I usually use for this recipe. It is great with the Rocamadour cheese and is available in many specialty bread bakeries around the country (a high-quality dense country bread will do). Cabécou de Rocamadour is by far my favorite goat cheese, especially when I can get it in the spring and perfectly ripe. This cheese is produced in the Midi-pyrénées region of France. The cheeses are shaped into small disks, which are perfect to melt onto a piece of toasted bread. If you can not find Cabécou de Rocamadour you can substitute any fresh young log-shaped chèvre. Cut off one-ounce slices and use in the same manner as the Cabécou de Rocamadour. (See Sources for the bread and the cheese.)

SERVES 6

6 1/2-inch-thick slices pain levain

Extra-virgin olive oil

1 teaspoon fleur de sel

6 1-ounce individual Cabécou Rocamadour cheeses

Preheat the broiler to high. Place the sliced pain levain on a baking sheet and brush lightly with the olive oil. Sprinkle the slices with the fleur de sel. Place one cheese in the center of each slice of bread. Place the pan under the broiler at least 6 inches from the heat, and broil until the cheese begins to bubble on top and the edges of the toast become golden brown, about 2 minutes. Serve warm.

STRAWBERRIES MACERATED WITH MOSCATO D'ASTI

Requires 1 hour advance preparation

When strawberries show up at your farmer's market in the late spring—small, sweet, ripe, and perfumed—it is the moment to make this refreshing recipe. Moscato d'Asti, an Italian sparkling wine, reminds me of the taste of fragoline, Italian wild strawberries.

SERVES 6

2 pints fresh strawberries, hulled and halved lengthwise

1 teaspoon superfine sugar

1 bottle (750 ml) Moscato d'Asti, chilled

Place the sliced strawberries in a nonreactive bowl and sprinkle with the sugar. Refrigerator for an hour before serving.

To serve, divide the strawberries among 4 serving bowls. Pour $1/2$ cup of the Moscato d'Asti into each bowl. Serve immediately. Serve the remaining Moscato d'Asti in glasses along with the strawberries.

The nine lives of a pasta recipe

CELERY, FENNEL, AND PARMIGIANO–REGGIANO SALAD
GARGANELLI EGG PASTA WITH LEMON AND BASIL
LITTLE CLOUDS

Cats have nine lives, and recipes have a lot more than that. Through how many hands have most recipes passed? I for one am not shy about asking for the recipe of something I have eaten and enjoyed. Even if you know a dish well, and have made it many times, you can discover a new twist, a secret ingredient, or a secret technique you never new about. As recipes are passed along, they always change, a bit like gossip—by the time you hear the story it has taken on more spice and flavor.

That's the case with this recipe for pasta with lemon. The first time I tasted it was in the south of France. I then encountered it several times in Italy, then in Ronkonkoma, Long Island. Although different, all the versions were good, and the lemon rind always played the starring role. In fact, I gave my version to a friend, who cooked it for her friend, who ended up describing it in the NEW YORK TIMES, where it took on yet another twist.

CELERY, FENNEL, AND PARMIGIANO-REGGIANNO SALAD

Requires 1 hour advance preparation

The key to this recipe is to make sure the celery and fennel are very chilled, crisp, and dry before dressing.

Using a vegetable peeler or paring knife, gently strip off the stringy fibers from the celery stalks. Slice the celery crosswise on the diagonal ⅛-inch thick (you should have about 2 cups). Line a bowl with slightly damp paper towels and place the celery in the bowl. Slice the fennel in half. Remove the core and slice lengthwise very thinly. Add the fennel to the celery and cover the vegetables with a slightly damp paper towel, then plastic wrap, and refrigerate for at least 1 hour.

MEANWHILE, MAKE THE VINAIGRETTE: Put the champagne vinegar, lemon juice, extra-virgin olive oil, and salt in a jar with a tight-fitting lid. Shake well. Reserve.

When ready to serve, place the celery, fennel, and shaved cheese in a large mixing bowl. Shake the vinaigrette well and add it to the bowl. Toss the salad gently, and then divide it evenly among 6 serving plates. Drizzle a little olive oil over each salad and then top with the parsley and pepper to taste. Serve immediately.

SERVES 6

5 stalks celery, ends trimmed

1 fennel bulb (about 8 ounces), washed and trimmed

4 ounces Parmigiano-Reggiano, shaved into thin slices

Extra virgin olive oil

¼ cup flat leaf parsley leaves, washed and patted dry, coarsely chopped

Freshly ground pepper

VINAIGRETTE

2 tablespoons champagne vinegar

Freshly squeezed juice of ½ lemon

3 tablespoons extra-virgin olive oil, plus more for drizzling

1 teaspoon sea salt

GARGANELLI EGG PASTA WITH LEMON AND BASIL

This pasta dish is my standby when I have unexpected guests and nothing in the refrigerator. I usually add something green to it, such as fava beans, basil, or arugula.

When cooking pasta it is important to use plenty of water. My formula is 6 quarts of water to one pound of pasta. Never add olive oil to the water—it coats the pasta and does not allow it to cook properly. And I follow the advice once given to me by a great Italian cook: Always toss a little of the cooking water with the finished pasta at the last moment to lend a nice consistency to the sauce. See Sources if you can't find gargenelli pasta locally.

Put the lemon zest and lemon juice in a large mixing bowl.

In a large pot of boiling salted water cook the pasta for 9 minutes or until al dente. Drain the pasta immediately and reserve ¼ cup of the cooking water. Add the drained pasta to the lemon mixture and toss well, then add the olive oil and toss. Slowly stir in the reserved pasta water. Add the crème fraîche, Parmigiano, and basil, and toss again. Season with the salt and the black and red pepper to taste. Serve immediately with extra Parmigiano.

SERVES 4 TO 6

Finely grated zest of 1 lemon

1 tablespoon lemon juice

8.8 ounces dried garganelli egg pasta (about 4 cups)

1 tablespoon olive oil

3 tablespoons crème fraîche

½ cup freshly grated Parmigiano, plus more for serving

¼ cup basil leaves, washed and patted dry, coarsely chopped

1 teaspoon salt

Freshly ground black pepper and crushed red pepper to taste

Freshly ground black pepper

LITTLE CLOUDS

2 to 3 hours cooking time

Franco Martinetti is one of the great winemakers in the Piedmont. His Barbera d'Asti, Montruc is justly famous. When we met, I discovered that he is as passionate about food as he is about wine. Franco took me to a local restaurant, Da Guido, to introduce me to classic regional dishes at their very best. When the meal was over we were served a tray of small white cream-filled meringue cookies. After such a big dinner I thought I could easily pass them by, but Franco insisted I try one. It melted in my mouth, and I could not stop with one. Franco's son, Sergio, had nicknamed them "Little Clouds" because they are so light. What is more perfect than that?

MAKES 4 DOZEN

Unsalted butter, for greasing
Cornstarch, for dusting
5 egg whites (about 3/4 cup), room temperature
1/8 teaspoon cream of tartar
1 1/2 cups superfine sugar
1 cup heavy cream, chilled
3 tablespoons confectioners' sugar

Preheat the oven to 110 degrees. Line 2 baking sheets with parchment paper. Lightly rub the parchment sheets with unsalted butter, and then lightly dust with cornstarch.

In a large bowl, beat the egg whites and cream of tartar until stiff, about 2 minutes. Add the sugar slowly to the egg white mixture and continue beating until stiff, glossy peaks form, about 5 minutes.

Place half the mixture in a pastry bag with a 1/4 inch tip. Pipe out 1-inch meringue rounds, 1/2-inch apart, onto the prepared baking sheets.

Place the meringues in the oven and bake until they're firm to the touch, lift off the parchment easily, and dry underneath, about 1 hour and 10 minutes. Open the door of the oven for 10 seconds every 15 minutes while baking to release any built up moisture and help the meringues stay dry and crisp.

Remove the meringues from the oven. Slide the meringues still on their parchment onto a wire rack to cool. When the baking sheets are cool, line them with new parchment and repeat the process until all of the meringue mixture has been used.

In a medium bowl, whip the heavy cream and the confectioners' sugar until thick. Peel all the meringues off the parchment sheets and place on a dry work surface. Turn 24 meringue halves upside down and make 2 rows of 12. Spoon the whipped cream into a pastry bag and pipe out approximately 1 teaspoon of whipped cream in the middle of each meringue. To assemble, take the remaining meringues and place one on top of each meringue to make sandwiches. Press each sandwich together gently.

Place each cookie in an individual paper pastry cup and refrigerate until serving. The Little Clouds will keep refrigerated for up to 3 days in a tightly covered container.

SUMMER

They say tomahto, I say tomato

GRILLED LOBSTER WITH CURRY SAUCE

CORN AND RICOTTA PUDDING

HEIRLOOM TOMATO SALAD WITH BASIL AND EXTRA-VIRGIN OLIVE OIL

FIG GALETTE

At least once every summer I try to visit my friend Dominique Browning, the editor of HOUSE & GARDEN. She has a wonderfully private Rhode Island house near everything you want in summer: a beautiful landscape, the ocean, fresh lobsters, a great farm stand with local corn and tomatoes, and the best homemade ice cream shack. Hers is a picture perfect New England summer community, and I find myself worrying about what I'm wearing to the farm stand even though I don't know a soul there. But underneath the proper exterior, this is a community of people who know how to celebrate the summer's bounty and love a good cocktail.

Dominique enjoys gathering friends together for lunch on a summer's day. There is nothing more pleasant than sitting outdoors in her garden and gazing at the water with good food and refreshing wines—looking forward to an afternoon of swimming at the beach to work it all off. Rhode Island summers are made for corn, tomatoes, and lobsters. Here are a few favorite recipes from lunches along the Ocean State's shores.

GRILLED LOBSTER WITH CURRY SAUCE

Requires 1 hour advance preparation

I prefer steaming lobster because the lobster meat is much more tender than when boiled. It is important that your lobster pot (see note below) is large. Otherwise the lobsters will not steam evenly. If your pot cannot hold all 6 lobsters at one time, cook them in batches.

SERVES 6

CURRY SAUCE

1 stick (4 ounces) unsalted butter
1 serrano chile, sliced in half
2 cloves garlic, chopped
2 tablespoons grated fresh ginger
2 tablespoons chopped basil
1 tablespoon curry powder
3 tablespoons maple syrup
2 tablespoons tamari sauce
1 teaspoon sea salt
½ cup heavy cream

LOBSTER

2 bottles of beer (12 ounces each)
6 1½ pound lobsters
Olive oil, for brushing
½ cup fresh basil leaves, coarsely chopped

MAKE THE CURRY SAUCE: Melt the butter in a saucepan over medium-high heat. Add all the other ingredients except the heavy cream. Simmer for 5 minutes. Add the cream and simmer for 5 more minutes, stirring occasionally. Remove from the heat and reserve.

COOK THE LOBSTER: In a large lobster pot, bring 2 inches of salted water and the 2 bottles of beer to a boil. Add all the lobsters, cover, and steam over high heat for 12 minutes. Remove the lobsters with tongs. When they are cool enough to handle, slice them in half lengthwise. Clean each half under running water, keeping the lobster meat intact. Arrange the lobster halves cut side up on a baking sheet. Lightly brush olive oil over the lobster meat.

Heat your grill. Place the lobsters, cut side down, on the grill, cover, and cook for 10 minutes. Turn the lobsters over and brush about 1 tablespoon of the curry sauce evenly over each of the lobster halves. Continue grilling, covered, for 2 more minutes. Place the lobsters on a serving platter. Heat the remaining curry sauce and brush over the lobster halves. Garnish with the basil and serve immediately.

Note: If you do not have a lobster pot you can place a steamer in a large pot to steam them.

CORN AND RICOTTA PUDDING

When making this recipe I like to use an earthenware or ceramic baking dish, which I can bring to the table and serve from.

SERVES 6 TO 8

4 tablespoons unsalted butter
3 shallots, diced
kernels from 6 ears of fresh sweet corn (about 4 cups)
4 medium eggs
1 cup fresh ricotta cheese
1 cup heavy cream
1 tablespoon chopped fresh chives
2 teaspoons sea salt

Preheat the oven to 350 degrees. Butter a 2-quart baking dish.

In a skillet, melt the butter over medium-high heat. Add the shallots and cook for 1 minute. Add the corn kernels and cook for 2 to 3 minutes, stirring constantly. Remove the pan from the heat, and pour the corn mixture into a bowl. When slightly cool, add the eggs, one at a time. Then stir in the ricotta cheese, heavy cream, chives, and salt. Pour the mixture into the prepared dish and bake for 30 minutes. Remove the pudding from the oven and let it rest uncovered for 5 minutes before serving.

HEIRLOOM TOMATO SALAD WITH BASIL AND EXTRA-VIRGIN OLIVE OIL

Many wonderful heirloom tomatoes fell by the wayside after World War II because their odd shapes and colors were not commercially appealing. Well, times have certainly changed. There are now dozens of varieties being grown, one more delicious than the next: Brandywine, Hillbilly, Sungold, Green Zebra, and Sweet 100's. With so many heirloom tomatoes available at farmer's markets across the country, it's easy to prepare this visual feast of a salad. I often let my tomatoes sit out several days to insure peak ripeness and I never refrigerate them. Use the highest quality extra-virgin olive oil for this salad.

Slice all the tomatoes crosswise ¹/₄-inch thick. Arrange layers of tomatoes and basil leaves on a serving platter. Drizzle the olive oil evenly over the tomatoes and basil. Sprinkle with the sea salt and freshly ground pepper. Serve immediately.

SERVES 6 TO 8

2 pounds assorted heirloom tomatoes
1 cup basil leaves, washed and dried
¹/₄ cup extra-virgin olive oil
2 teaspoons coarse sea salt
Freshly ground black pepper

FIG GALETTE

Requires 3½ hours advance preparation

Galette is a French term for an open-faced tart baked with flaky pastry and fruit. It's my idea of a perfect dessert for all seasons, but especially in the summer months when galettes can be filled with apricots, cherries, and peaches. When figs are in season, they are my favorite fruit to bake in a galette—they practically explode with flavor.

I like to make enough dough for two galettes so I can either make one larger galette, or save some extra dough in my freezer.

MAKE THE DOUGH: Whisk the flour, sugar, and salt in a mixing bowl, until well combined. Add the butter and, with your fingers, gently work the butter and flour together until the mixture resembles coarse cornmeal. Add 5 tablespoons of the ice water and continue working the dough until it begins to come together. Add more water, a half a tablespoon at a time if needed. Divide the dough in half and shape each half into a small disk. Gently flatten the disks. Wrap each disk in plastic wrap and refrigerate for 2 hours or up to 4 days (or freeze for up to 1 month).

Remove one disk from the refrigerator and let it soften for 10 minutes. Unwrap it and on a lightly floured surface, roll it out into a 12-inch round. Place an 11-inch plate over the dough and trim off the edges of the pastry with a small knife. Transfer to a parchment-lined baking sheet, and refrigerate for 30 minutes.

MAKE THE FILLING AND ASSEMBLE THE TART: Preheat the oven to 350 degrees. Remove the galette dough from the refrigerator. Starting at the center of the pastry, place the fig halves cut side up in concentric circles, leaving a 1-inch border free of fruit. Sprinkle 2 tablespoons of sugar over the figs. Cut 2 tablespoons of the butter into little pieces and scatter over the figs. Rotating the galette, fold the dough border over itself, crimping and pushing it up against the outer circle of fruit. Sprinkle the lavender evenly over the figs.

Melt the remaining 1 tablespoon butter and brush the crust with the melted butter. Sprinkle the remaining 1 tablespoon sugar over the melted butter.

Place the tart in the oven and bake until the edges are golden brown, 40 to 45 minutes. Remove from the oven and dust with confectioners' sugar. Serve warm with vanilla ice cream.

SERVES 6

Makes 2 9-inch galettes

DOUGH

2 cups all-purpose flour

1 teaspoon sugar

¼ teaspoon salt

1½ sticks (6 ounces) cold unsalted butter, cut into small pieces

5 tablespoons ice water

FILLING

1 pound fresh figs, stems removed, halved

3 tablespoons granulated sugar

1 tablespoon plus 2 teaspoons unsalted butter

1 teaspoon fresh lavender, coarsely chopped

Confectioners' sugar, for dusting

Vanilla ice cream, for serving

Fish and chips

BEER-BATTERED COD

FRENCH FRIES WITH FINES HERBES

FRIED OYSTERS WITH YELLOW PEPPER REMOULADE

CHICKPEA PANISSES

TEMPURA-BATTERED ZUCCHINI BLOSSOMS

PANNA COTTA WITH BLUEBERRY SAUCE

I have never met anyone who did not like fried food. But if you are like me, you probably never fry food at home because you can't get rid of the smell or the grease. My solution is to fry outdoors. I use a piece of equipment called the Fisherman's Friend (see Sources). It is a free-standing, stainless steel burner which hooks up to a butane gas tank. It's easy to set up and use, but be careful, hot oil is dangerous.

Be sure to use a good oil. Different oils produce different results. Peanut oil is best for potatoes, batter-fried foods, and fish because it can sustain a high temperature without burning and its flavor is not overpowering. Olive oil can also withstand high heat and I use extra-virgin for frying vegetables and chicken when I want the olive flavor to come through—though using a lot of it gets expensive, so use it sparingly. Olive oil and peanut oil, once cooled and drained through cheesecloth, can be reused once before discarding.

These recipes can also be made on your stove of course. Once you get started, you will try it again and again, and come up with many variations of your own. I guarantee it.

BEER-BATTERED COD

When frying, start with fresh fish—the texture and flavor of frozen fish will just not be as good. I use cod for this recipe because the flesh stays moist and firm after frying. You can substitute any firm white-fleshed fish. Use this batter also when frying shrimp and scallops. A fine sea salt and malt vinegar are the only embellishments needed—and french fries on the side, of course (recipe follows).

In a large bowl, sift the flour and salt together.

Gradually stir in the beer and then the ice water.

In a 4-quart cast-iron or enameled saucepan, heat the peanut oil to 350 degrees.

Place several pieces of cod in the batter and turn to coat both sides of the fish. Lift the fish from the batter and allow any excess batter to drip back into the bowl. Gently place the batter-coated fish into the hot oil and fry each side for 1 minute, until golden brown. Using tongs, transfer the fish to paper towels to drain. Make sure the oil comes back to 350 degrees before adding more cod. Fry the remaining fish in the same manner.

Drizzle the vinegar over the fish and sprinkle with salt to taste. Serve two pieces per person.

SERVES 6

2 cups self-rising flour

1 teaspoon fine sea salt, plus more for sprinkling

1/2 cup cold beer

1 cup ice water

2 quarts peanut oil

1 1/4 pounds fresh cod, cut into 2-ounce pieces

Malt vinegar

FRENCH FRIES WITH FINES HERBES

Requires 1 hour advance preparation

French fries should be firm and crisp. To accomplish this, fry the potatoes twice and in small batches. Small batches prevents the temperature from dropping too quickly and overcooking the potatoes. I fry them once ahead of time and then again once I have fried my fish. Also, I make sure the raw potatoes are completely dry before adding them to the hot oil, because moisture will cause splattering.

Peel the potatoes and slice into strips, 1/8 inch lengthwise and then 1/8 inch crosswise. Place the sliced potatoes in cold water.

When ready to fry, drain the potatoes in a colander. Place the potatoes on a kitchen towel and pat dry thoroughly. Line a baking sheet with paper towels.

In a 6-quart cast-iron or enameled saucepan, at least 5 inches deep, heat the oil to 350 degrees. Fry the potatoes in three batches, making sure that before each addition the oil is 350 degrees. Cook each batch for approximately 2 minutes or until the potatoes are golden brown and rise to the top. Then use a large slotted spoon or a mesh strainer

SERVES 6

5 pounds russet potatoes

2 quarts plus 1 cup peanut oil

1 tablespoon each chopped fresh rosemary, thyme, and sage

1/4 cup flat-leaf parsley leaves

2 teaspoons sea salt

to transfer them to the baking sheet lined with paper towels.

Increase the heat of the oil to 375 degrees. Line another baking sheet with paper towels.

When ready to serve, fry the once-cooked potatoes in three batches, checking to maintain an oil temperature of 375 degrees before each addition. Fry the potatoes for 2 minutes or until golden brown and crisp. Remove with a large slotted spoon or mesh strainer and place them on to the baking sheet lined with paper towels.

Place the rosemary, thyme, sage, and parsley in a large bowl and mix with the salt. Add the potatoes and toss with the herbs. Serve immediately.

FRIED OYSTERS WITH YELLOW PEPPER REMOULADE

Requires 1 hour advance preparation

We made these fried oysters daily at my restaurant and served them with the remoulade, which is a lovely accompaniment to all kinds of fried fish. The oysters are also great simply with salt and freshly squeezed lemon juice.

MAKES 2 DOZEN

REMOULADE

1 yellow bell pepper
1½ cups mayonnaise, preferably homemade
1 shallot, peeled and minced (about 2 tablespoons)
Grated zest and juice of 1 lemon
¼ cup parsley leaves, coarsely chopped
1 tablespoon fresh chives
1 tablespoon chopped fresh tarragon
1 teaspoon sea salt
Freshly ground black pepper

OYSTERS

24 medium oysters, shucked
2 cups whole milk
1 cup all-purpose flour
1 teaspoon sea salt
⅛ teaspoon freshly ground white pepper
1 teaspoon cayenne pepper
1 quart peanut oil

MAKE THE REMOULADE: Place a baking rack over a burner on your stovetop, then place the pepper directly on it. Cook the pepper on high heat until the skin is completely black, using kitchen tongs to continually turn the pepper, about 10 minutes. Place the pepper in a plastic bag and seal. When the pepper is cool enough to handle, remove from the bag. Using a paper towel rub off the blackened skin from the pepper (do not rinse the pepper). Slice it in half lengthwise and remove the seeds. Wipe out any remaining seeds with a paper towel.

Slice the pepper lengthwise into ⅛-inch strips and then crosswise into ⅛-inch slices.

Place the sliced pepper into a mixing bowl along with all the remaining ingredients. Mix until well blended. Cover and refrigerate for one hour.

FRY THE OYSTERS: In a nonreactive bowl, combine the oysters and the milk. Cover and refrigerate for 1 hour. Line a platter with several layers of paper towels and set aside.

Combine the flour, salt, and the white and cayenne peppers in a bowl. Remove the oysters from the refrigerator. Drain them in a colander and place several at a time in the flour mixture. Turn to coat both sides generously with the flour and place them on a large plate. Continue until all the oysters are coated.

In a heavy 4-quart saucepan heat the peanut oil heat to 350 degrees.

Add 6 oysters and fry until the oysters are golden brown and float to the top, 2 to 3 minutes. Using a slotted metal spoon, transfer the oysters to the paper-towel lined platter. Fry the remaining oysters, 6 at a time, making sure the oil returns to 350 degrees before each addition. Season with salt and freshly ground pepper to taste and serve immediately with the yellow pepper remoulade.

CHICKPEA PANISSES

Requires 2 hours advance preparation

Panisses are a wonderful chickpea fritter, a recipe that originated from the port of Marseille back in the sixteenth century. Though the classic shape when served in Marseille is a flat round discs, most often they are made into shapes of French Fries. The most memorable Pannisses I ever had were served at Chez Panisse's 30th-year anniversary celebration. It was an incredible outdoor lunch for 400 guests on the Campanile Esplanade at the University of California at Berkely. They were frying them in large skillets outdoors and serving them warm with just a little sea salt sprinkled on top. I also love freshly ground pepper as a garnish and to sip chilled rosé along with them.

MAKES APPROXIMATELY 32 PANISSES
1 quart water
2 cups plus 2 tablespoons extra-virgin olive oil
1¾ cups chickpea flour, sifted
1 teaspoon sea salt
Sea salt and freshly ground white pepper

Lightly oil a 12-by-9-inch baking pan.

Put the water and 2 tablespoons of the olive oil in a large saucepan and bring to a boil. Using a whisk, slowly whisk the chickpea flour into the boiling water until all the flour is incorporated, then whisk in the salt. Reduce the heat and continue to cook, stirring, for 10 minutes. The mixture should be firm but not solid. Remove from the heat and press the mixture into the lightly-oiled pan, smooth the top. Set aside uncovered for 2 hours or up to 12 hours.

Slice the panisses into 3- by 1-inch rectangles. Line a large platter with paper towels.

Pour 2 cups of extra-virgin olive oil into a large cast-iron skillet or casserole with sides and heat to 355 degrees over medium-high heat.

Using a metal spatula, transfer as many panisses from the pan to the skillet as can fit without crowding. Fry for about 1 minute on each side until golden brown. Reheat the oil to 355 degrees before adding more panisses. Using a slotted metal spoon, transfer the panisses to the paper towel-lined platter. Sprinkle with the salt and pepper and serve warm.

TEMPURA-BATTERED ZUCCHINI BLOSSOMS

If you have a garden and can pick the flowers just before cooking, that's best. You can fry the blossoms before they are fully opened, but if already open, make sure they are firm and not limp or bruised.

In a small bowl, beat the egg for 1 minute. Add the ice cubes and the cold water and mix together. Put the flour in a separate bowl, make a well in the flour and add the egg mixture. Mix together lightly, just until the batter is evenly moist (the ice cubes keep the batter cold and will eventually melt). Do not over beat.

Line a large platter with paper towels.

In a large skillet with sides at least 2 inches high, heat the olive oil over medium-high heat.

Place two zucchini blossoms in the batter, turning to coat them completely. Then place them in the hot oil. Fry for approximately 1 minute on each side, until golden brown. Remove the cooked blossoms from the skillet and place them on the plate lined with paper towels. When all the zucchini blossoms have been fried, place them on a serving platter and sprinkle them with salt and freshly ground white pepper to taste. Garnish with the lemon wedges and serve immediately.

SERVES 6

1 large egg

3 ice cubes

1/2 cup cold water

1 1/2 cups all-purpose flour, sifted

1 cup extra-virgin olive oil

6 firm zucchini blossoms

Sea salt and freshly ground white pepper

1 lemon, cut into 6 wedges

PANNA COTTA WITH BLUEBERRY SAUCE

Requires 4 hours advance preparation

In summer, chilled panna cotta is a refreshing alternative to ice cream.

MAKE THE PANNA COTTA: Grease six 4-ounce tumblers or ramekins with the butter and place them on a baking tray. Put the gelatin in a large mixing bowl and gently stir in 1/4 cup of the milk. Set aside.

Place the cream, remaining 1/4 cup milk, and the confectioners' sugar in a saucepan and bring to a boil. Immediately turn off the heat. Stir well. Slowly pour the contents of the pan into the gelatin mixture, whisking constantly until cool. Stir in the vanilla. Divide the mixture among the molds. Cover and refrigerate for at least 4 and up to 24 hours.

MAKE THE BLUEBERRY SAUCE: Rinse the blueberries in a colander. Remove any visible stems. Combine the blueberries, sugar, and water in a saucepan. Bring to a boil, stirring to dissolve the sugar. Reduce the heat and simmer for 2 minutes. Remove from the heat and let cool. Puree the mixture in a blender until smooth.

Dip the tumblers one at a time into hot water and then turn them out onto serving dishes. Pass the blueberry sauce separately.

MAKES 6 INDIVIDUAL DESSERTS

PANNA COTTA

2 teaspoons softened unsalted butter, for coating the tumblers

1 envelope unflavored gelatin (2 1/2 teaspoons)

1/2 cup whole milk

1 cup heavy cream

1/2 cup confectioners' sugar

1/2 teaspoon vanilla extract

BLUEBERRY SAUCE

1 1/2 cups fresh blueberries

1/4 cup sugar

1/4 cup water

A working gardener's lunch

GRILLED TUNA NIÇOISE PLATTER
GRILLED GARLIC BREAD RUBBED WITH TOMATO
PAVLOVA WITH SEASONAL BERRIES

At the height of the summer, it's hard to relax if you have a garden. There is always something to do. And if there isn't something to do, there is something to plan. But what could be better than sitting in your garden and enjoying it by having a long leisurely lunch?

On a warm summer's day I like my lunch to be light yet satisfying, and I love to have a glass of wine to go with it. I often drink a chilled young Chinon, a dry red wine from the Loire that works well with tuna, such as the Tuna Niçoise in this menu. At other times I choose a chilled Arneis, a crisp white wine from the Piedmont region of Italy with a hint of effervescence.

This menu is dedicated to all those accomplished gardeners out there who create beautiful spaces for the rest of us. Most of the food can be prepared in advance and assembled at the last minute so you have plenty of time to take in the glories of the garden.

SERVES 6

CAPER VINAIGRETTE

2 tablespoons capers, rinsed, drained, and finely chopped

2 tablespoons chopped shallots

4 teaspoons sherry vinegar

Freshly squeezed juice of 1 lemon

1/2 cup extra-virgin olive oil

Sea salt and freshly ground black pepper to taste

TUNA NIÇOISE

6 1/4-pound tuna fillets (about 1-inch thick)

2 tablespoons olive oil

3/4 pound small new potatoes, washed

1 teaspoon sea salt, plus more for seasonings

1/2 pound green beans, washed and ends trimmed

Freshly ground black pepper to taste

1/4 pound mixed garden lettuces, washed and dried

6 hard-boiled eggs, peeled and sliced in half lengthwise

12 oil-packed anchovy fillets in oil, drained on paper towels

2 ripe avocados

1/4 pound Niçoise olives

1/2 pound assorted cherry or pear tomatoes

1 tablespoon capers, rinsed and drained

1 lemon, cut in sixths

Requires 1 hour advance preparation

I always look forward to making a Tuna Niçoise. Everytime I make it, it changes a little, and you'll also find it's easy to substitute whatever you might have on hand. Sometimes I pan-sear the tuna if I don't have time to set up a grill, sometimes I add roasted peppers or large tomato slices, and sometimes I don't even use salad greens, just vegetables. You can use whatever is available in your kitchen—a helpful thing for those of us who didn't have time to shop because we were so busy working in our gardens.

MAKE THE VINAIGRETTE: Combine the capers, shallots, vinegar, and lemon juice in a bowl. Whisk in the olive oil. Then add salt and pepper.

MAKE THE TUNA NIÇOISE: Rinse the tuna and pat dry. Place on a plate and brush both sides with the olive oil. Cover with plastic wrap and refrigerate until ready to grill. Return to room temperature 1/2 hour before grilling.

Place the potatoes in a saucepan with one teaspoon salt, and cover with cold water. Bring the water to a boil and cook over medium-high heat, until tender when pierced with a sharp knife, about 15 minutes. Drain in a colander and reserve.

In a large saucepan of boiling, salted water, cook the green beans for 5 minutes or until al dente. Prepare a large bowl of ice water while the beans are cooking. Drain the beans in a colander and immediately plunge it into the ice water for 1 minute. Drain the beans, and let dry on paper towels.

Heat your grill. Season the tuna with salt and pepper. Grill the fillets for 3 minutes per side for medium-rare or 4 minutes per side for well done. Slice the tuna diagonally 1 inch thick. Line a platter evenly with the garden lettuces. Arrange the sliced tuna in the center of the platter. Place the egg halves on each corner of the platter. Place 1 anchovy across each egg half. Place the green beans along one side of the tuna. Slice the potatoes in half and place them on the other side of the tuna. Slice the avocados in quarters and remove the peel. Place the avocado slices evenly around the platter. Sprinkle the niçoise olives, tomatoes, and capers over the entire salad. Place the lemon wedges on either end of the platter. Drizzle half the vinaigrette dressing over the salad, and pass the rest separately.

GRILLED GARLIC BREAD RUBBED WITH TOMATO

Heat your grill. Slice the bread into ¹/₂-inch diagonal slices. Brush both sides with the olive oil and lay the sliced bread on a baking sheet. Grill both sides of the bread until golden brown and remove from the heat. When the bread is cool enough to handle, rub the garlic onto the bread. Slice the tomato in half crosswise and rub the tomato over the bread slices. Let the tomato juices soak in. Sprinkle all the toasts with the salt, then place the toasts on the grill with the flavored side down. Grill for approximately 1 minute. Remove from the grill and serve at once.

SERVES 4 TO 6

¹/₂ pound hearty rectangular loaf French Bread

¹/₃ cup extra-virgin olive oil

1 clove garlic, peeled

1 very ripe tomato (about ¹/₂ pound)

2 teaspoons sea salt

bricco delle ciliegie

roero arneis
denominazione di origine controllata

1989

Imbottigliato all'origine dall'Azienda Agricola
Almondo Giovanni
Montà d'Alba - Italia - Alcohol 12% by vol.

Product of Italy   IMPORTED BY ROBERT CHADDERDON SELECTIONS   750 ML
                     NEW YORK, N.Y.

PAVLOVA WITH SEASONAL BERRIES

SERVES 6 TO 8

Vegetable oil, for greasing

1 tablespoon arrowroot or cornstarch, plus more for dusting

1 cup superfine sugar

4 egg whites, at room temperature

¼ teaspoon cream of tartar

1 teaspoon distilled white vinegar

1 teaspoon vanilla extract

1 cup heavy cream, chilled

2 tablespoons confectioners' sugar, sifted, plus more for dusting

2 cups assorted fresh berries such as blueberries, red and golden raspberries, currants, and blackberries

4 mint sprigs, for garnish

Requires 1 hour advance preparation

A traditional pavlova is made with passionfruit, but in the height of berry season, what better compliment to the firm shell and soft interior of a pavlova.

Fresh eggs are essential for a good meringue. To test an egg for freshness, place it in a glass and fill it with water. If the egg sits horizontally, it's fresh. If it stands on its end, it isn't. Humidity softens a meringue's shell, so avoid making it on a humid day.

Preheat the oven to 400 degrees. Line a baking sheet with parchment paper. Lightly grease the parchment paper with vegetable oil and dust with cornstarch.

Mix ¼ cup superfine sugar with 1 tablespoon arrowroot and set aside.

Using an electric mixer, beat the egg whites and cream of tartar (with the whisk attachment, if possible) at high speed until soft peaks form. Reduce the speed and slowly beat in the remaining ¾ cup sugar 1 tablespoon at a time. Then add the sugar-arrowroot mixture, 1 tablespoon at a time. When the meringue is firm and glossy, beat in the vinegar and vanilla. Using a rubber spatula, turn the meringue onto the center of the parchment and shape it into an oval, approximately 10 inches by 7 inches. With a spoon, make a bowl-like indentation in the center, leaving a border approximately 2 inches wide.

Put the meringue in the oven and immediately reduce the temperature to 250 degrees. Bake for 45 minutes. Turn off the oven and let the meringue remain inside for an additional 30 minutes. Remove the meringue from oven and let cool completely on a wire rack.

In a medium bowl, whip the heavy cream until soft peaks form. Stir in 2 tablespoon of the confectioners' sugar. Place the meringue on a serving platter and fill the indentation with the whipped cream. Top with the berries and mint sprigs and dust with additional confectioners' sugar. Serve immediately.

A sandwich to go or stay

RADISHES, SWEET BUTTER, AND SALT ON A BAGUETTE

EGG SALAD ON GARLIC TOAST

CHICKEN, ARUGULA, AND GREEN MAYONNAISE ON CIABATTA

NOT-JUST-YOUR ORDINARY GRILLED CHEESE: FRESH MOZZARELLA
WITH TOMATO CONFIT

PEEL-THE-TOMATO BLT WITH AVOCADO

THE BEST LOBSTER ROLL

OPEN-FACED ROSE GERANIUM POUND CAKE SANDWICH
WITH STRAWBERRIES IN GERANIUM SYRUP

Thank you John Montagu, Earl of Sandwich, for your great invention. No matter what time of day it is, a sandwich makes the perfect meal. Over the years, I have had my fair share of sandwiches both high and low. Among the latter, was a potato Po-Boy I was encouraged to order in a New Orleans dive. What arrived was a giant roll slathered in mayonnaise and filled with french fries. A local specialty, maybe, but not for me.

At the other end of the spectrum was the most elegant array imaginable from Harry's Bar in Venice—a plate of perfectly sculpted sandwiches with crusts removed and cascading waves of chicken salad down their centers.

To me sandwiches are not about using leftovers or foods you grab when you are in a hurry. That's not to say that I don't think leftover grilled steak or chicken makes a good sandwich, but I prefer filling mine with the best of the season. To make a good sandwich you have to layer the textures and flavors that compliment each other, but you also need to keep it simple. And sandwiches are meant to be eaten as soon as they are made.

When it comes to a picnic, you can make sandwiches in many combinations by bringing the ingredients with you and assembling them on the spot. And if you are really ambitious, there are many sandwiches you can make on the grill.

If a picnic is a memory, then the sandwich is a souvenir.

RADISHES, SWEET BUTTER, AND SALT ON A BAGUETTE

Requires 1 hour advance preparation

This sandwich is my standby cocktail sandwich in the summer when young radishes are small, sweet, and slightly bitter. It is so easy to put together, makes for a beautiful presentation, and guests love them.

Refrigerate the radishes for 1 hour before serving.

Arrange the radishes, butter, and a bowl of sea salt on a large platter along with a chopping board. Let guests slice their own bread and create their own open-faced sandwich. Have an extra bowl on hand for the discarded radish stems.

SERVES 8

2 bunches fresh baby radishes, washed, stems intact

Sweet French butter, at room temperature

Sea salt

1 baguette

EGG SALAD ON GARLIC TOAST

A good egg salad is hard to beat and it is also hard to resist the temptation to throw in a lot of different ingredients. When I make egg salad I like it simple—fresh eggs, good mayonnaise, and finely minced shallots—and served on garlic toast. A must with this sandwich is cournichons or gherkins.

When boiling eggs always use salted water, which prevents the shells from cracking.

Place the eggs in a large pot, cover with cold salted water, and bring to a boil. Reduce the heat and simmer the eggs for 5 minutes.

Drain the eggs in a colander and rinse with cold water until cool. Peel the eggs.

Chop the eggs and place in a large bowl along with the shallots, mayonnaise, salt, and freshly ground pepper to taste. Mix well. Cover and refrigerate the salad until ready to use.

To make the sandwiches, toast the bread until golden brown. Place the toasts on a chopping board and brush one side with the olive oil. Rub the garlic over the olive oil and sprinkle with salt. Spread approximately 1/2 cup of the egg salad on each toast. Sprinkle with the chopped parsley. Slice the toasts in half. Serve immediately along with a bowl of cornichons or gherkins.

MAKES 8 OPEN-FACED SANDWICHES

12 fresh large eggs, at room temperature

2 shallots, minced (about 1/4 cup)

1/2 cup mayonnaise, preferably homemade

2 teaspoons sea salt, plus more for sprinkling

Freshly ground white pepper to taste

8 1/2 inch-thick slices hearty French bread (approximately 7 inches by 3 inches)

Extra-virgin olive oil, for brushing

1 clove garlic, peeled

1 tablespoon chopped fresh parsley

Cornichons or gherkins, for serving

CHICKEN, ARUGULA, AND GREEN MAYONNAISE ON CIABATTA

Requires 2 hours advance preparation

When I am in the mood for some serious comfort food, a chicken sandwich is almost always on the top of my list. It brings back memories of childhood. Once at the Borough Hall Market, a wonderful indoor/outdoor farmer's market in London, a vendor was making this sandwich. Though all the ingredients seemed simple enough, it was like no other chicken sandwich I have tasted. It hit me why: The chicken was just roasted and served warm. The vendor had organic chickens turning in a rotisserie, and he pulled the white and dark meat off the bones. Within minutes he was making the sandwich.

MAKE THE MAYONNAISE: Wash the parsley, basil, and spinach. Pat dry. Place the mayonnaise and greens in a blender or food processor and puree for 30 seconds. Refrigerate until ready to use (the mayonnaise is best made 1 day ahead so the herbs have time to infuse).

MAKE THE SANDWICHES: Preheat the oven to 375 degrees. Wash the chicken and pat it dry. Rub the chicken inside and out with the salt and pepper to taste. Place it, breast side down, on a rack inside a roasting pan just large enough to hold the chicken snugly. Place the pan in the oven and bake the chicken for 40 minutes. Using kitchen tongs, turn the chicken over and continue roasting for another 40 minutes.

Meanwhile, cut the stems from the arugula and discard. Soak the leaves in a bowl of water for 30 minutes, tossing several times to remove the grit. Remove the arugula from the water and pat or spin dry. Wrap in paper towels and refrigerate until ready to assemble the sandwich.

Remove the chicken from the oven and let cool. Remove and discard the chicken skin. Remove the legs and thighs and using your fingers, pull the meat off the bones and shred. Cut the breasts off the bone and use your fingers to shred the breast meat.

Remove and shred any remaining meat left on the carcass. Place all the chicken meat in a bowl and toss the chicken meat with salt and pepper to taste. Reserve.

To assemble the sandwich, cut each loaf of ciabatta into 4 equal pieces then slice each piece in half horizontally. Place the halves of ciabatta, sliced side up, and spread as much of the green mayonnaise as desired on each slice. Layer the chicken meat evenly across the bottom slices of ciabatta. Top evenly with the arugula. Place the top ciabatta slice on the arugula. Cut into eighths and serve immediately.

MAKES 8 SANDWICHES

GREEN MAYONNAISE

1/4 cup flat-leaf parsley leaves
1/4 cup basil leaves
6 spinach leaves, coarsely chopped
1 cup mayonnaise, preferably homemade

SANDWICHES

One 2- to 2 1/2-pound whole chicken
2 teaspoons sea salt, plus more for seasoning
Freshly ground black pepper
1/4 pound fresh arugula
2 loaves Ciabatta (about 1 pound)

NOT-JUST-YOUR-ORDINARY GRILLED CHEESE: FRESH MOZZARELLA WITH TOMATO CONFIT

I prepare tomato confit to get a more concentrated tomato flavor. In the summer I always keep a jar of tomato confit in my refrigerator, for moments just like this. If you do not have time to make the tomato confit, substitute with very ripe tomatoes.

MAKE THE CONFIT: Prepare a large pot of boiling water. Slice an "X" through the skin across the back of each tomato and plunge into the boiling water for 2 minutes. Remove the tomatoes from the water and run under cool water to stop the cooking. Peel each tomato and cut into quarters. Using a sharp knife cut along the inside of each quartered tomato to remove the seeds.

Preheat the oven to 250 degrees. Generously brush a baking sheet with some of the olive oil. Place the tomatoes, cut side down, on to the baking sheet. Brush the tops with the remaining olive oil. Bake for 1 hour. Remove from the oven and let cool. Place the tomatoes in a nonreactive bowl, and pour any excess olive oil over them. (The tomatoes can be stored in the refrigerator for up to 2 weeks.)

MAKE THE SANDWICHES: Lay the sourdough bread in two rows on a chopping board. Spread the mayonnaise evenly on each slice. Top the bottom row of bread with half the sliced mozzarella. Place 2 slices of tomato confit, then 2 basil leaves over the cheese. Sprinkle the salt over the tomato and basil. Top all the sandwiches with the remaining mozzarella cheese then top with the remaining slices of bread. Trim off all the crusts. Butter both sides of each sandwich with the butter.

Place a large skillet over medium heat. Place the sandwiches in the skillet, reduce the heat to medium-high, cover, and cook for 5 minutes on each side. (To cook the sandwiches evenly turn every 2 minutes.) Remove the sandwiches from the skillet and let rest for 1 minute. Slice in half and serve warm.

MAKES 4 SANDWICHES

TOMATO CONFIT

4 medium tomatoes, ripe but firm
1/2 cup extra-virgin olive oil

SANDWICHES

8 slices white sourdough sandwich bread
1/4 cup mayonnaise
1/2 pound fresh unsalted mozzarella, thinly sliced
8 large basil leaves, washed and patted dry
1/2 teaspoon sea salt
3 tablespoons unsalted butter, softened

PEEL-THE-TOMATO BLT WITH AVOCADO

This is a sandwich to eat as close to the frying pan as possible because the bacon should be warm. And to give it just the right texture, the tomato should always be peeled. Avocado is a good addition to this sandwich, but purists can leave it out.

In a medium saucepan, boil enough water to completely cover the tomato. Slice an "X" through the skin across the back of the tomato. When the water is boiling, add the tomato and boil for 1 minute. Remove the tomato from the water and run under cool water to stop the cooking. Peel the tomato and slice crosswise into $1/4$-inch thick slices, set aside.

Preheat the oven to 200 degrees. Heat a skillet large enough to cook all the bacon at once. Fry the bacon until golden brown and crisp, but do not overcook. Put the bacon on a plate lined with paper towels and place in the preheated oven until ready to assemble the sandwiches.

Toast the bread and lay it on a chopping board. Spread the mayonnaise evenly on all of the slices. Fold the romaine leaves in half and place on 4 pieces of the bread. Slice the avocado in half lengthwise, discard the pit and then slice the avocado into quarters. Remove the peel and slice each quarter into thin slices. Place a sliced avocado quarter on each of the romaine leaves.

Season the avocado with salt and pepper. Place 3 slices of the warm bacon on each sandwich. Cover with the top slice of bread, and slice the sandwiches in half. Serve immediately.

MAKES 4 SANDWICHES

1 ripe tomato (about $1/2$ pound)

12 slices smoked bacon (see Sources)

8 slices Pain de Mie, or any dense white bread

$1/4$ cup mayonnaise

4 fresh romaine lettuce leaves, washed and patted dry

1 ripe avocado

Sea salt and freshly ground black pepper to taste

THE BEST LOBSTER ROLL

One summer, I ate several dozen different lobster rolls traveling through Maine. After that trip, I decided that my favorite lobster roll was the most obvious: A toasted buttered hot dog bun filled with the freshest possible lobster meat.

To insure the freshest meat you need to start with live lobsters (see Sources for mail-order lobster). See page 60 for the best technique for steaming lobsters. In New England they sell special hot dog buns just for lobster rolls. The sides are cut off which makes it easy to fry. I improvise by just slicing $1/4$ inch off the rounded top of a normal hot dog bun.

Slice the lobster tail in half, rinse, and cut into 1-inch slices. Remove the cartilage from the claws and slice the claw meat into

MAKES 1 LOBSTER ROLL

About $1/4$ pound cooked lobster meat (from a 1-pound lobster)

1 hot dog bun, $1/4$ inch sliced off the top

2 tablespoons unsalted butter, melted, plus extra for dipping

Mayonnaise, for serving

Potato chips, for serving

thirds. Slice the remaining lobster meat into 1-inch slices. Using several layers of paper towels pat the lobster meat dry.

Using a pastry brush, coat the inside and the outside of the bun with the melted butter. Heat a skillet and toast the bun until light brown, about 1 minute per side.

Remove the bun from the skillet and place it on a serving plate. Fill with the lobster meat. Brush the lobster meat with any remaining melted butter. Serve with sides of melted warm butter and mayonnaise. Garnish with potato chips.

OPEN-FACED ROSE GERANIUM POUND CAKE SANDWICH WITH STRAWBERRIES IN GERANIUM SYRUP

SERVES 9

ROSE GERANIUM SUGAR
12 rose geranium leaves
1 pound sugar

STRAWBERRIES IN ROSE GERANIUM SYRUP
1 cup sugar
3/4 cup cold water
6 rose geranium leaves
(about 1/2 ounce total)
1 drop therapeutic grade geranium oil
(optional)
1/2 pound ripe strawberries

POUND CAKE
1 cup cake flour
1 teaspoon baking powder
1/4 teaspoon plus 1 pinch sea salt
1 cup unsalted butter, at room temperature
2 drops geranium oil (if rose geranium sugar is not available)
1/4 cup heavy cream
1 teaspoon vanilla extract
1 teaspoon finely grated orange zest
4 large egg whites, at room temperature

GARNISH
1 cup heavy cream, chilled
Rose geranium leaves, for garnish

Requires 7 days advance preparation time if making geranium sugar
The subtle infusion of rose geranium leaves in this recipe takes me back in time. Rose geranium, *pelargonium graveolens*, has been used in culinary preparations for centuries. If rose geranium leaves are not available you can substitute geranium oil (See Sources), which is distilled from the leaves. The oil is very concentrated so use it sparingly.

MAKE THE GERANIUM SUGAR: Place 2 geranium leaves in a tight-fitting 1-quart glass jar and pour some sugar over them. Repeat this process until all the rose geranium leaves and sugar have been used. Cover tightly and store in a cool dark place for 7 days. Before using, sieve the sugar and discard the geranium leaves. (You will need 1 cup plus 1 tablespoon rose geranium sugar for this recipe. Reserve the remainder for another use.)

MAKE THE STRAWBERRIES IN SYRUP: In a saucepan, combine the sugar, water, and geranium leaves over medium heat. Gently bring to a boil for 2 minutes; then turn off the heat. Let the syrup cool, then pour it through a strainer and discard the geranium leaves. Add the geranium oil, if using. Reserve.

Wash and hull the strawberries and slice them lengthwise into 1/8-inch slices. Put them in a nonreactive bowl and add the cooled geranium syrup. Cover and let macerate for 2 hours at room temperature. Then cover and refrigerate until ready to use.

MAKE THE POUND CAKE: Preheat the oven to 350 degrees. Grease and flour a 9-by-5-inch loaf pan.

Sift the cake flour, baking powder, and 1/4 teaspoon salt into a large bowl. Set aside. Using an electric mixer, beat the butter until creamy, 1 to 2 minutes, then gradually add 1 cup of the rose geranium sugar. Continue beating until light and fluffy, about 5 minutes. Mix in the geranium oil if using.

With the mixer set at low speed alternately add the flour mixture and cream in 3 parts, scraping the sides of the bowl as necessary. Beat in the vanilla and orange zest.

In a separate bowl, beat the egg whites with the remaining pinch of salt at high speed (with a whisk attachment, if possible) until soft peaks form, about 1 minute. Using a large rubber spatula, gently fold the egg whites into the batter. Pour the batter into the prepared pan. Bake for 40 minutes or until a cake tester inserted in the center of the cake comes out clean. Remove the cake from the oven and let cool in the pan for 15 minutes. Run a thin knife around the sides of the cake and invert it. Let the cake cool right side up on a baking rack.

In a large bowl, combine the heavy cream and 1 tablespoon of the rose geranium sugar. Beat until the cream is thick and forms stiff peaks.

To assemble, slice the pound cake into 9 slices. Place them on a large serving platter or on individual serving plates. Top each slice with a spoonful of whipped cream and then several spoonfuls of the strawberries along with some of their syrup. Garnish with geranium leaves.

A bonfire on the beach

BISTECCA FIORENTINA A.K.A. TUSCAN STEAK

FRESHLY PICKED, GRILLED WHITE CORN ON THE COB

BEET AND CUCUMBER SALAD WITH FRESH MINT, ALMONDS, AND
ORANGE VINAIGRETTE

DOWNTOWN BAKERY GINGERSNAP COOKIES

HOT CHOCOLATE WITH ROASTED MARSHMALLOWS

Since I can't afford to live by the water, I've found that the next best thing is eating by it. There is something magical about a meal by the ocean at the end of a summer's day when it's still light at 9:00 or 10:00 in the evening. The sound of the waves, the smell of the fire, an array of tempting food, and a cooler full of wine really bring out your appetite.

When I was spending summers in East Hampton, my friends Greg and Katherine would have splendid bonfire dinners on the shore. Everyone brought a dish and we grilled several things on the fire. On one occasion a friend scrambled eggs and dates as a first course. Another brought homemade ice cream with her own caramel sauce and we made sundaes for dessert. We finished one meal with hot chocolate and roasted marshmallows. People who didn't cook brought wine or firewood. There really aren't any rules for assembling a meal like this and the surprises are a big part of the fun. The best part of the event is that no one gets stuck doing dishes all night. Everyone just packs up their stuff and heads home.

The star attraction of this menu is the steak and there are a few simple sides. Feel free to improvise to your heart's content.

A word of warning: If you are building your fire on a rocky beach be aware that some rocks can explode if they over heat. Also, check to see if you need fire permits for your local beach.

BISTECCA FIORENTINA A.K.A. TUSCAN STEAK

SERVES 6

2 1½ -inch thick porterhouse steaks (about 3 pounds each)
¼ cup olive oil
2 lemons, halved crosswise
Sea salt and freshly ground black pepper to taste

When I make this recipe I use Porterhouse steak. T-bone is a good substitute—it is the same cut as the porterhouse without the tenderloin attached. Also, I find that meat that has been aged at least three weeks has the best flavor. Bring the meat to room temperature before grilling to insure that it will cook through properly. I always add the olive oil and seasonings after I have cooked and sliced the steak so I can really savor their flavor.

Usually I drink a Bordeaux with steak, but in the summer with my Bistecca Fiorentina I like to pour a rosé from Bandol, preferably Domaine Tempier. It's full-bodied and has the muscle to hold up to the grilled meat, yet it has great finesse and is cool and refreshing.

Heat your grill and grill rack. Place the steaks on the rack and grill, partially covered, for 5 minutes per side for rare, 6 to 7 minutes for medium rare, and 8 to 9 minutes for well done. Remove the meat from the grill and let rest for 10 minutes before slicing. Slice the meat off the bone, then slice diagonally into ½-inch slices. Place the sliced steak on a platter, drizzle with the olive oil, and squeeze the lemons on top. Season with salt and pepper and serve.

FRESHLY PICKED, GRILLED WHITE CORN ON THE COB

SERVES 6

12 ears fresh white corn, picked that day
3 limes, cut in quarters
Sea salt

Requires 2 hours advance preparation

Freshly picked white corn at the height of the season is so good you could almost eat it raw. My simple method is to soak the whole ear—cornhusk and all—in water just before grilling. When you grill the corn, the water steams the corn and cooks it just enough to bring out the sweetness. Then just pull off the husks, squeeze some lime juice on the corn, sprinkle with some salt, and serve.

Trim 2 inches off the stem of each corn and remove one layer of the husk. Cut the tops of the corn and remove the brown silk.

Place the corn in a large bucket and fill with water. The corn should be completely submerged. Soak the corn for at least 2 hours before grilling.

Heat your grill. The embers should be quite hot. Remove the corn from the water and shake off any excess water. Place all the corn on the grill, or cook it in several batches if necessary. Turn the corn every 2 minutes until the husks are golden brown all over—approximately 6 minutes. Remove the corn from the grill, peel off the husks, and serve the corn immediately with lime wedges and sea salt.

BEET AND CUCUMBER SALAD WITH FRESH MINT, ALMONDS, AND ORANGE VINAIGRETTE

Requires 1 hour advance preparation

SERVES 8

2 pounds small beets (about 2 ounces each), stems removed

¼ cup extra-virgin olive oil, plus more for drizzling

¼ cup raw almonds

Finely grated zest and juice of 1 orange

3½ tablespoons red wine vinegar

½ teaspoon fleur de sel (see page 28), plus more for sprinkling

¼ cup tightly packed fresh mint leaves

3 kirby cucumbers, peeled and thinly sliced

Freshly ground pepper to taste

This is a great salad to bring on a picnic. I prepare it at home and assemble it when I arrive. It is a nice contrast to the steak and corn because of the combination of textures and flavors. It also makes a beautiful presentation.

Preheat the oven to 350 degrees. Wash the beets well and place them in a large bowl. Add 2 tablespoons of the olive oil and toss. Use parchment paper to line a roasting pan just large enough to hold the beets in one layer. Add the beets, cover the pan tightly with aluminum foil, and bake for 1 hour or until tender when pierced with a sharp knife. Remove the foil. When the beets are cool enough to handle, peel them. Slice the beets into very thin slices and reserve.

Place the almonds on a baking sheet and bake in the preheated oven for 10 minutes or until golden brown. Remove, and when cool enough to handle, chop the nuts into rough pieces.

In a small bowl, mix together the orange zest and juice, vinegar, and ½ teaspoon fleur de sel. Slowly whisk in the remaining 2 tablespoons olive oil, and set aside.

Slice the mint leaves into a chiffonade: Take 4 to 5 leaves at a time, pile them one on top of another, and roll them together as if making a cigar. Finely slice the roll crosswise. Continue in the same manner until all the mint has been sliced.

Place the beets and cucumber slices on a platter or divide among individual serving dishes. Whisk the orange vinaigrette, then drizzle over the beets and cucumbers. Sprinkle the salad with fleur de sel and some freshly ground pepper. Scatter the almonds and mint chiffonade on top. Drizzle with olive oil and serve.

DOWNTOWN BAKERY GINGERSNAP COOKIES

Requires 1 hour advance preparation

Ever since childhood I have loved gingersnaps for their intense flavor. In fact, I have often used them as a litmus test of a bakery's excellence. In 1990, when I was in Healdsburg, California, I visited the Downtown Bakery and Creamery and discovered the best gingersnap I had ever tasted. In subsequent years I made sure to make as many pilgrimages as I could to that bakery. Eventually the owner, Kathleen Sullivan, began selling her cookie dough frozen and I was able keep it on hand. More recently I got the recipe and since then I have made my own, baking several batches at a time. My only change to her recipe is the addition of freshly grated ginger for a little extra punch.

Sift together the flour, baking soda, cinnamon, baking powder, and salt, set aside.

Using an electric mixer, beat the butter and sugar together until light and fluffy, approximately 4 minutes. Add the eggs one at a time and mix briefly between additions. Add the vanilla. Scrape down the sides of the bowl with a rubber spatula. Add the molasses and mix well. Scrape the sides again. Add the two gingers and mix until well incorporated. Add the dry ingredients in four additions, mixing well after each addition. Cover the bowl with plastic wrap and refrigerate for approximately one hour, or until well chilled. Take the dough out of the bowl and divide it in half. Roll each piece into an 8-inch log. At this point you can slice the dough or wrap it in plastic wrap and freeze for later use. (Before slicing the frozen dough, let it stand at room temperature for 5 to 10 minutes to soften.)

Preheat the oven to 350 degrees. On a lightly floured surface, slice the cookies a scan 1/4-inch thick. Place them 1 inch apart on ungreased cookie sheets. Sprinkle each cookie lightly with sugar. Bake for 10 minutes or until the cookies have puffed and then fallen and the tops have cracked. Let cool on wire racks. The cookies can be stored in an airtight container for up to 5 days. For longer storage, freeze.

MAKES 6 DOZEN

3 3/4 cups all-purpose flour

1 tablespoon baking soda

2 teaspoons cinnamon

1 1/2 teaspoons baking powder

1/2 teaspoon salt

2 sticks (1/2 pound) unsalted butter, cut into 2-inch pieces

1 1/2 cups sugar, plus more for sprinkling

2 eggs, at room temperature

1/2 teaspoon vanilla extract

1/3 cup light molasses

2 tablespoons freshly grated ginger

1 tablespoon ground ginger

HOT CHOCOLATE WITH ROASTED MARSHMALLOWS
The hot chocolate can be made ahead of time and reheated.

Dissolve the cocoa powder in 1 cup of the milk. Combine the mixture, the remaining milk, the chocolate, and the sugar in a large saucepan. Stir over low heat until the chocolate is melted and thoroughly blended and the hot chocolate is heated through.

Spear one or two marshmallows on the end of a long skewer. Place over an open fire or your stovetop and cook until golden brown.

To serve, fill 6 mugs 3/4 full with the hot chocolate. Place a roasted marshmallow on top and serve warm.

SERVES 6

1/4 cup unsweetened cocoa powder

5 cups whole milk

6 ounces dark chocolate, broken into 1/4 inch pieces

1/2 cup sugar

6 large marshmallows

Dinner for summer's end

CORN SOUP WITH LIME, CILANTRO, AND AVOCADO

GRILLED CHICKEN MARINATED IN RED WINE, THYME, AND GARLIC

PUREED POTATO AND FENNEL GRATIN

SKILLET-GRILLED HARICOTS VERTS WITH LEMON AND EXTRA-VIRGIN OLIVE OIL

ROASTED PEACHES WITH CARDAMOM SUGAR AND MASCARPONE SAUCE

The days of eating outdoors are numbered, the last of the tomatoes and corn are at the farm stand, and we'll soon be back to our busy fall schedules. The odd thing is that to my mind one of the best summer months is September, but we don't always enjoy it enough because we've ended the season too early. In September the ocean is finally warm, the crowds are gone, there are plenty of great berries still to be picked, and I can put up enough tomatoes to last until next summer. How bad is that?

Somehow I become a little more serious by September and want to cook a little differently then. I came up with this menu when I was trying new ways to eat corn and chicken. I love grilled corn on the cob but I thought a soup would make a nice change as the nights got cooler. I was craving Coq au Vin so I decided to make a marinade for the chicken out of the usual ingredients and then grill it instead of stewing it. As for all those amazing fruits, well, roasted peaches are perfect for summer-going-on-fall too.

CORN SOUP WITH LIME, CILANTRO, AND AVOCADO

Using a small sharp knife, scrape the corn kernels from the cobs into a bowl. Scrape the milk from the cobs into the bowl of corn with the back of a knife.

In a large stockpot, bring the water to a boil and add the corn cobs. Cook over medium-high heat for 30 minutes. Remove the pot from the heat, discard the cobs and reserve the corn stock. You should have 5 cups.

In a medium stockpot, melt the butter over medium-high heat. Add the shallots and garlic and cook for several minutes. Add the corn kernel milk mixture, potatoes, and corn stock. Bring to a boil, reduce the heat, and cook over medium-high heat for 20 minutes. Add the salt. Remove the soup from the heat and let cool. Puree in a blender.

Return the soup to the stockpot, bring to a high simmer, and stir in the lime zest, lime juice, and 1 tablespoon of the cilantro.

Pour the soup into individual bowls, garnish with the avocado and remaining cilantro leaves.

SERVES 6 TO 8

6 ears of white corn, husks reserved
8 cups water
2 tablespoons unsalted butter
2 shallots, diced (about 4 tablespoons)
2 cloves garlic, thinly sliced
1 cup 1/2-inch diced potato
2 teaspoons sea salt
Finely grated zest of 1 lime
Freshly squeezed juice of 2 limes
2 tablespoons chopped fresh cilantro
1 ripe avocado, peeled and diced into 1/4 cubes

GRILLED CHICKEN MARINATED IN RED WINE, THYME, AND GARLIC

Requires 12 hours advance preparation

In a large, nonreactive bowl, layer the chicken alternately with a mixture of the thyme and garlic. Drizzle with 1/3 cup of the oil and then add enough wine to cover the chicken completely. Cover the bowl and refrigerate for 12 to 24 hours.

Remove the chicken from the refrigerator 1 hour before grilling. Heat your grill. Remove the chicken pieces from the marinade and place them on the hot grill. Cook, turning frequently, until done, about 12 minutes per side. Transfer the pieces to a serving platter, as soon as they are done and brush with extra olive oil.

SERVES 6

2 3-pound chickens, cut into 8 pieces each
2 bunches fresh thyme
1 head of garlic, peeled, and thinly sliced
1/3 cup extra-virgin olive oil, plus more for brushing
Approximately 2 bottles hearty red wine like Cotes du Rhone (750 ml each)

Crema di mascherpone

1 etto mascherpone

1 uovo

1 cucchiaio di tavola
   zucchero

rhum o Cognac

tuorlo colla zucchero
   insieme → crema
poi il mascherpone
   mescolato bene

bianco a neve
   unire tutto
aggiungere il liquore

Malè 30/12/84   Franco Colombani

PUREED POTATO AND FENNEL GRATIN

SERVES 6

2 pounds Yukon gold potatoes, peeled and quartered

3 fennel bulbs (about 2 pounds), peeled and cut lengthwise into sixths

1 onion, peeled and quartered

2 cloves garlic

1 stalk celery, sliced into 2 inch pieces

2 teaspoons sea salt, plus more for seasoning

¼ cup heavy cream

3 tablespoons unsalted butter, cut into ¼-inch pieces

Freshly ground white pepper

This puree is a perfect match with the chicken. I always use a food mill to puree potatoes (see Sources). The potatoes come out much lighter and the ingredients are thoroughly integrated.

Place the potatoes, fennel, onion, garlic, celery, and 1 teaspoon salt in a large stockpot. Cover with cold water and bring to a boil over high heat. Reduce the heat to medium, partially cover, and cook until the potatoes and fennel are tender, 30 to 35 minutes.

Drain the vegetables in a colander. When cool enough to handle, put all the ingredients through a food mill set over a large bowl. Stir in the cream and 2 tablespoons butter until well incorporated. Season with 1 teaspoon of the salt and pepper to taste.

Preheat the oven to 350 degrees. Butter a 12-inch oval or gratin dish and add the puree. Top with the remaining 1 tablespoon butter. Cover and bake for 20 minutes. Uncover and serve immediately.

SKILLET-GRILLED HARICOTS VERTS WITH LEMON AND EXTRA-VIRGIN OLIVE OIL

SERVES 6

1 pound haricots verts, stem ends trimmed and tail ends intact

2 tablespoons extra-virgin olive oil, plus more for drizzling

2 cloves garlic, peeled and smashed

Freshly squeezed juice from ½ lemon

1 teaspoon fleur de sel (see page 28)

Even though the French translation for haricots verts is simply green beans, they are much thinner than regular green beans. This recipe works best using the thinnest beans available. By using a skillet on a grill you are able to sear and brown the beans quickly. You can make this recipe on your stovetop as well, but be aware that, without a vent over your stove, the kitchen will get quite smoky. This recipe can be made in advance and served at room temperature.

In a 4-quart saucepan of boiling, salted water, cook the beans for 4 minutes. Prepare a large bowl with ice water to chill the beans. When the beans have cooked, drain them in a colander and immediately plunge them into the ice water. When cool, drain in the colander.

Heat your grill. Place a 12-inch skillet on the hot grill, cover the grill and let the skillet heat up for 5 minutes. Add the oil and garlic. Cook the garlic, turning several times, until lightly golden brown and remove. Add the beans and spread them across the skillet in a single layer. Cook the beans for 2 to 3 minutes, turn over and cook for 2 to 3 minutes longer, until seared and lightly brown. Add the lemon juice, toss and cook until all the lemon juice evaporates, about 1 minute. Using tongs, transfer the beans to a large platter. Sprinkle the fleur del sel over the beans, then drizzle lightly with more olive oil.

ROASTED PEACHES WITH CARDAMOM SUGAR
AND MASCARPONE SAUCE

Requires 2 hours advance preparation

The spicy flavor of cardamom is a wonderful complement to the sweetness of the ripe peaches. Since most ground spices sold are old and have lost their vibrant flavor, I always grind my own. Cardamom seeds removed from their pod are sold in most Middle East specialty stores (see Sources).

I like to serve the peaches with a sauce made from mascarpone cheese, a dense, buttery-rich triple cream cheese. It is the Italian version of English double cream. When eating at Albergo De Sole, in Maleo, Italy, the chef/owner Franco Colombani graciously gave me this recipe after I told him how much I loved it. Later I discovered that mascarpone is made in that region of Italy.

When purchasing eggs that will be used raw, buy the best organic eggs available. Bring to room temperature right before making the sauce, then refrigerate the sauce until ready to serve.

MAKE THE MASCARPONE SAUCE: In a medium bowl, beat the egg yolks and sugar with a whisk or an electric beater until light and fluffy, about 2 minutes. Beat in the mascarpone.

In a separate bowl, whip the egg whites until stiff but not dry, 3 to 4 minutes. Fold the egg whites and cognac into the mascarpone mixture until incorporated. Refrigerate the sauce for 2 hours before serving.

MAKE THE ROASTED PEACHES: Preheat the oven to 375 degrees. Butter a large ceramic or glass-baking dish.

Bring a large pot of water to a boil. Cut an "X" through the skin at the bottom of each peach. Plunge the peaches in the boiling water for 30 seconds. Remove the peaches from the water and place in a bowl of cold water to keep them from cooking. When the peaches are cool enough to handle, cut them in half, remove the pits and then peel off the skins.

Place the peaches cut side down in the prepared dish. Squeeze the lemons over the peaches. Sprinkle the butter over the peaches. Combine the sugar and ground cardamom and then sprinkle the mixture over the peaches. Add the sauterne to the dish. Cover the dish and bake the peaches for 30 minutes.

Place two peach halves cut side up on each of 6 serving dishes. Spoon the extra juice from the baking dish over the peaches. Spoon some mascarpone sauce over each peach and serve warm.

SERVES 6

MASCARPONE SAUCE

2 eggs, separated, at room temperature

2 tablespoon sugar

1 cup mascarpone cheese

2 tablespoons cognac or rum

ROASTED PEACHES

6 ripe peaches (about 3 pounds total)

2 lemons, cut in half

2 tablespoons unsalted butter, cut in ¼-inch dice

½ cup sugar

1½ teaspoons cardamom seeds, finely ground in a spice grinder or mortar

½ cup sauternes wine

AUTUMN

It's my birthday and I'll cook what I want to

CAESAR SALAD WITH GARLIC CROUTONS
FRESH DUNGENESS CRACKED CRAB WITH AIOLI
DUNGENESS CRAB CAKES WITH MASHED POTATO TARTAR SAUCE
SOURDOUGH BREAD WITH SWEET BUTTER
MEYER LEMON COCONUT CAKE

Maybe I love having this menu for my birthday because it reminds me of my childhood in San Francisco when my Dad would take my brothers and me to Fishermans' Wharf for Dungeness crab. It also reminds me of going to a restaurant with my family and watching the waiter mix a Caesar salad on a cart right in front of our table. But maybe I just love it because when it's my birthday, I want to eat what I want to eat at home with my friends instead of going to one more restaurant and ending up a little disappointed because the meal isn't perfect. This is one of my favorite menus because I don't have to spend hours in the kitchen, and I know it will be delicious! Even though I live in New York City, I can have the cooked crab shipped overnight and it will be as fresh as if I went to the wharf to buy it. I always have a good loaf of sourdough bread and some sweet butter to go with the crab. That's part of the tradition too.

Since one night of Dungeness crab isn't enough for me, I always order extra and get my friends to help pick out the meat so I can make crab cakes the next day. Basically, the whole point here is to get a huge Dungeness crab fix until next autumn.

CAESAR SALAD WITH GARLIC CROUTONS

Requires 1 hour advance preparation

Crisp chilled romaine lettuce and chilling the plates one hour before serving is one of my trademarks when I serve a Caesar salad.

SERVES 6

CROUTONS

6 1-inch-thick slices sourdough bread
About ¼ cup extra-virgin olive oil
2 cloves garlic, peeled
2 teaspoons sea salt

CAESAR DRESSING

1 large egg, at room temperature
Freshly squeezed juice of ½ lemon
1 clove garlic, peeled and minced
1 tablespoon red wine vinegar
1 teaspoon Worcestershire sauce
3 oil-packed anchovy fillets, finely chopped
Three dashes Tabasco sauce
½ teaspoon sea salt, plus more for seasoning
½ cup extra-virgin olive oil
½ cup freshly grated Parmigiano cheese
Freshly cracked black pepper to taste

SALAD

2 heads romaine lettuce
2 tablespoons coarsely chopped flat-leaf parsley

MAKE THE CROUTONS: Preheat the oven to 350 degrees. Brush both sides of each bread slice with olive oil. Place the bread in a single layer on a baking sheet and bake for 10 minutes. Turn over and bake for another 10 minutes. Remove from the oven and when cool enough to handle, rub both sides of each bread slice with the garlic. Tear the bread into 1-inch pieces or cut into 1-inch cubes. Place the bread back on the baking tray and bake until golden brown, 5 to 10 minutes. Remove from the oven, sprinkle with the salt, let cool, and reserve. You should have approximately 2 cups.

MAKE THE CAESAR DRESSING: Place the egg in boiling water for 2 minutes. Rinse in cold water and break into a small bowl. Add the lemon juice, garlic, vinegar, Worchester sauce, anchovies fillets, Tabasco, and salt, and whisk to combine. While whisking, slowly pour in the olive oil until well blended and the dressing slightly thickens. Stir in half of the grated Parmigiano cheese. Season with salt and pepper to taste. Refrigerate until ready to use.

PREPARE THE SALAD: Tear off and discard the outer leaves from the romaine lettuce until you get to the pale inner leaves. Cut off and discard 2 inches from the top of the remaining leaves and discard the stem. You should have 1½ pounds of leaves total. Place the leaves in a bowl of cold water for 10 minutes. Remove them from the water, shake off excess water, pat dry, and wrap in paper towels or a tea towel. Refrigerate for 1 hour or up to 24 hours.

Remove the lettuce from the refrigerator. Tear the leaves into large pieces and place in a large salad bowl. Add the croutons. Whisk the dressing and then pour three quarters of it over the salad. Toss to coat. Divide the salad among 6 chilled individual serving plates and sprinkle the remaining Parmigiano cheese and the parsley evenly over the salads. Drizzle the remaining dressing over the salads.

FRESH DUNGENESS CRACKED CRAB WITH AIOLI

My formula is one crab per person. If you are having the crabs shipped to you, ask to have them cooked, cleaned, and cracked. If you have access to fresh, boil your own, as described here. To insure the pure flavor of the crab I add nothing to the water except salt. If I have access to seawater, I boil the crabs in that, adding no extra salt. It is important not to overcook the crab or the meat tends to toughen.

I serve the crabs with aioli, the French garlicky mayonnaise. If there ever was a time that you could experience the alchemy of cooking most fully, it is when making an aioli with a mortar and pestle (see Sources for mortars and pestle). You can also use an electric hand mixer, adding chopped garlic to the mixing bowl.

MAKE THE AIOLI: Place the garlic and salt in a mortar large enough to hold all the ingredients, and pound it to a smooth paste. Add the egg yolks and beat with the pestle until well combined. Tip for making aioli: Drip the oil from a teaspoon to begin the emulsion process to prevent the aoli from separating. Begin adding the oil, a few drops at a time, letting it run down the side of the mortar, beating continually until the mixture starts to thicken. The aioli mixture should begin to thicken immediately. Continue adding all the remaining oil slowly in a steady stream, always adding to the side of the mortar. If the ailoi becomes to thick to beat, add a few drops of Meyer lemon juice to thin it out. Then stir in the remaining Meyer lemon juice. Cover and refrigerate until ready to serve.

PREPARE THE CRABS: Wash the crabs under cold running water. Bring a large stockpot (at least 12 quarts) of water to a boil. Add the salt and 2 to 3 crabs. Return the water to a rapid boil, cover, and boil the crabs for 12 minutes. To test doneness, pull off a leg—the meat should be firm and white. Using tongs, remove the crabs from the boiling water, and rinse under cold water. Bring the water back to a boil and cook the remaining crabs in batches.

To clean the crabs, remove the top shell and then the gills on either side of the body. Rinse under cold running water. Turn the crabs over and remove the triangular piece off the breast body. Cut the crabs in half and tear off the legs. Place the crab pieces onto a large platter. If not serving immediately, cover the crab, and refrigerate. Serve chilled with the garlic aioli.

SERVES 6

AIOLI

2 cloves garlic, peeled

1 1/2 teaspoons coarse sea salt

3 large egg yolks, at room temperature

1 1/2 cups extra-virgin olive oil

2 tablespoons freshly squeezed Meyer lemon juice, for thinning

CRABS

6 2-to 2 1/2-pound live whole Dungeness crabs

2 tablespoons coarse sea salt

Requires 1 hour advance preparation

MAKES 8 CRAB CAKES

TARTAR SAUCE

1 cup mayonnaise, preferably homemade

1 small Yukon gold potato, baked, peeled, mashed, and cooled

¼ cup minced scallions

Finely grated zest of 1 lemon

1 tablespoon freshly squeezed lemon juice

1 tablespoon chopped fresh parsley

2 drops of Tabasco sauce or to taste

Sea salt and freshly cracked black pepper to taste

CRAB CAKES

1 pound Dungeness crabmeat or jumbo lump crabmeat, gently rinsed in cold water and patted dry

1 egg and 1 egg yolk, beaten together lightly

Finely grated zest of 1 lemon

2 teaspoons minced chives

5 tablespoons unsalted butter

1 cup plus 2 tablespoons unseasoned bread crumbs

3 tablespoons minced shallots

1 teaspoon salt

1 tablespoon olive oil

There is no way I can write this book and not include my recipe for crab cakes. Everyone who has had them loves them and they use to fly out the door at my restaurant. These crab cakes are not bread cakes which most people get when they order crab cakes. If you can't get Dungeness crabmeat, use jumbo lump. It is more expensive that regular crab but it is worth it. There are too many shells to clean out of the other, and usually it's not the prime meat. Since the cakes are rich, I always serve a tossed green leafy salad alongside.

MAKE THE TARTAR SAUCE: Mix all the ingredients in a small bowl until well combined. Cover and refrigerate for 1 hour. (I find the sauce is much better if it is made at least 12 hours before serving.)

MAKE THE CRAB CAKES: In a large bowl, gently fold together the crabmeat, eggs, lemon zest, and chives. Be careful not to break up the lumps of crabmeat. Reserve the mixture in the refrigerator. In a skillet, melt 3 tablespoons of the butter. Add 2 tablespoons of the breadcrumbs, the shallots, and salt, and cook over medium-high heat, stirring frequently, for 5 minutes. Remove from the heat, and let cool. When completely cool, add to the crabmeat mixture. Stir together gently, until well combined.

Pour the remaining 1 cup of unseasoned breadcrumbs onto a large plate or platter.

Fill a ⅓-cup measure with the crabmeat mixture and then empty it into your hand. Shape into a round cake and flatten slightly. Place the crab cake on the breadcrumbs to lightly coat one side, and then turn it over to coat the other side. Repeat this process until all the crabmeat mixture is used, placing the coated crab cakes on a platter until ready to use. (The crab cakes can be made to this point up to 6 hours ahead; cover and refrigerate.) In a large skillet, over medium-high heat, melt the remaining 2 tablespoon butter with the olive oil. Add the crab cakes, making sure they do not touch, reduce the heat to low, and cook, uncovered, until golden brown and firm to the touch, about 6 minutes on each side. To test for doneness, stick a knife in the center of a crab cake—if the knife comes out clean, they are ready.

MEYER LEMON COCONUT CAKE

Requires 4 hours advanced preparation

When it comes to my birthday cake, I want my two favorite ingredients—lemon and coconut. I live for the delicate yet tangy Meyer lemons, and luckily autumn is their season. They make the cake sour and sweet at the same time, and their zest gives it the perfect hit of citrus without being overpowering. If you don't have Meyer lemons don't let that stop you from making this cake.

And who says I have to blow out all the candles? I like to give everyone their own slice of cake with a candle and let them make a wish and ask for a blessing too.

MAKE THE CAKE: Preheat oven to 350 degrees. Butter two 9-inch-round cake pans. Line the bottoms with parchment paper and butter and lightly flour the lined pans.

In a large bowl, using an electric mixer, beat the butter and lemon zest until smooth. Gradually add 1 3/4 cups of the sugar and beat until fluffy, about 5 minutes. Add the eggs one at a time, mixing until well incorporated. With the mixer set on the lowest speed, combine the flour in three parts, alternating with the milk, mixing only until incorporated. Mix in 1/3 cup of the Meyer lemon juice until incorporated.

Divide the batter evenly between the two prepared pans. Bake for 25 to 30 minutes, or until a cake tester comes out dry. Let the cakes cool in their pans for 10 minutes. Remove and cool on a rack.

Meanwhile, place the remaining 1/2 cup Meyer lemon juice and remaining 1/4 cup sugar in a small saucepan, and heat, stirring until the sugar has dissolved. When the cakes have cooled, place top sides up on a piece of parchment paper. Prick the tops of the cakes all over with a fork and brush each cake with all of the hot glaze.

MAKE THE CREAM CHEESE FILLING: Using an electric mixer, beat the cream cheese and butter until smooth, about 2 minutes. Add the remaining ingredients and mix until well incorporated.

MAKE THE COCONUT ICING: Place all the ingredients except the coconut in a double boiler and bring the water to a rapid boil. Using an electric mixer, beat the mixture until the icing holds firm peaks, 6 to 8 minutes. Remove from the heat and mix in the coconut.

ASSEMBLE THE CAKE: Place one cake layer upside down on a large flat plate. Spread the cream cheese filling over the top of the cake. Place the other cake upside down on top of the filling, pressing the layers gently together. Using a pastry brush, dust off any loose crumbs on the cake. Ice the sides and then the top with the coconut icing.

SERVES 12 TO 15

CAKE

2 sticks (1/2 pound) unsalted butter, at room temperature, plus more for greasing

Finely grated zest of 2 Meyer lemons

2 cups sugar

4 large eggs, at room temperature

3 cups self-rising cake flour, sifted

3/4 cup milk

2/3 cup freshly squeezed juice from Meyer lemons

CREAM CHEESE FILLING

1/4 pound cream cheese

4 tablespoons unsalted butter, at room temperature, cut into 1/4-inch pieces

Finely grated zest of 2 Meyer lemons

1 tablespoon Meyer lemon juice

3/4 cup freshly grated coconut or packaged sweetened coconut

1 cup confectioners' sugar

COCONUT ICING

3 eggs whites, at room temperature

2 cups granulated sugar

Finely grated zest of 2 Meyer lemons

2 tablespoon corn syrup

1 1/2 cups freshly grated coconut or packaged sweetened coconut

A flight of wines . . . and serious jet lag

OYSTERS ON THE HALF-SHELL WITH MIGNONETTE SAUCE AND THINLY SLICED RYE
1995 RENE AND VINCENT DAUSVISSAT CHABLIS, FOREST

POULE AU POT WITH VEGETABLES AND SAUCE VELOUTÉ
JASMINE RICE WITH KAFFIR LIME LEAVES AND GARLIC
A FLIGHT OF ROBERT MONDAVI
CABERNET SAUVIGNON RESERVE, 1962, 1965, 1974, 1987, 1990, 1997

CHEESES
1990 QUNITARELLI AMARONE DELLA VALPOLICELLA

TARTE TATIN WITH CRÈME FRAÎCHE
1990 CHATEAU d'YQUEM
1995 CUILLERON CONDRIEU-AYGUETS

As soon as I became the food editor of HOUSE & GARDEN, I began campaigning for a wine column. I felt strongly that you couldn't cover food well unless you were willing to include wine. No sooner had I proposed the column than Dominique Browning, the magazine's editor, responded, "Jay McInerney—he's the perfect writer for it." I was dumbfounded. My anxiety rose as a lunch was arranged with the infamous Jay at the Four Seasons restaurant in New York. It didn't diminish when he arrived looking as if he'd been out all night.

Despite Jay's appearance, he surprised and impressed me at that lunch with his knowledge and enthusiasm for wine. I was even more impressed by his honesty and good nature. I began to see Dominique's point. Jay is a great stylist who can serve up his passions to the reader without snobbery or unnecessary technical detail. We have been working together now for five years and have become the best of friends. I love him dearly.

When Jay and I visit winemakers, I am especially interested in how they pair food with their wines. During our visit to the cellars of Francois Mitjavile in St. Emillion his wife, Miloute, taught me a great deal in this respect. Miloute made a poule au pot using an old hen she got from a neighbor in their village. Francois got some oysters nearby as a first course for which he poured one of his younger wines, A 1997 Tertre Routebouf. The wine went surprisingly well with them. Then we moved on to our main course. Miloute brought out a heaping platter filled with chicken, vegetables, rice, and a gravy made from the stock. Francois then started pouring older vintages of his wines and I saw that the simplest of foods are the best foil for the complexity of great Bordeaux.

SAUTERNES-APPELLATION CONTRÔLÉE

Château d'Yquem

Lur-Saluces

MIS EN BOUTEILLE AU CHÂTEAU

OYSTERS ON THE HALF-SHELL WITH MIGNONETTE SAUCE AND THINLY SLICED RYE

Requires 1 hour advance preparation

I like to test to see if my oysters are alive before eating them. Touch the edge of the oyster just after opening—if alive it should move. You can open the oysters up to one half hour prior to serving but no more than that. Always keep the oysters on a bowl of ice or in the refrigerator. Fanny Bay Oysters are delicious, but any seasonal oyster or a variety of them will do. (See Sources for oysters and oyster tools for shucking.)

When serving oysters, I like to offer a dense, light-rye bread thinly sliced. Rye, along with sweet butter is the best match to the brininess of the oysters—as are the mignonette sauce and fresh Meyer lemon wedges if available.

MAKE THE MIGNONETTE SAUCE: Combine all the above ingredients in a bowl and let sit for at least 1 hour before serving.

PREPARE THE OYSTERS: Fill a platter or bowl with crushed ice. Fill a small bowl with the mignonette sauce and place it in the center of the ice. Wedge the opened oysters snuggly in the ice around the sauce. Place the sliced rye on a plate on the side along with sweet butter and a bowl of lemons. Serve immediately.

SERVES 6

MIGNONETTE SAUCE

½ cup good-quality red wine vinegar
1 tablespoon minced shallots
Freshly cracked black pepper

OYSTERS

3 dozen Fanny Bay oysters
Thinly sliced dense light-rye bread
Sweet butter, for serving
2 Meyer lemons cut into quarters

POULE AU POT WITH VEGETABLES AND SAUCE VELOUTÉ

Requires 4 hours advance preparation

I know that the word fowl might send you into orbit. But a fowl simply means an older bird, which is what you need for this recipe so that you can make a rich enough stock. You won't achieve that with store-bought chicken because they are young, and when cooked for any length of time will fall apart. Using fowl allows you to cook the stock for a longer period of time, thus getting a richer deeper flavor, and still be able to serve the meat.

Many of us do have farmers' markets in our neighborhoods, and many farmer's markets have great poultry purveyors. Ask your purveyor if he can supply you with an older bird or substitute a farm-raised pheasant or a guinea hen (see Sources).

MAKE THE POULE AU POT: Cut the lemon in half and rub it all over the fowl. Put the water, veal bones, onion, garlic, and herbs in a 12-quart stockpot and bring to a boil. Add the fowl and return to a boil. Then reduce the heat and simmer, partially covered, for 3½ hours, or until the leg can easily be pulled from the joint.

Meanwhile trim all but 2 inches of the green from the leeks. Cut as much off the root ends as possible but not so much that the leeks will fall apart while cooking. Slice each leek in half lengthwise, and place the cut leeks in a large bowl of water for several hours. (Leeks are very sandy and it is important to give them time to soak so that the sand falls to the bottom of the bowl.) Remove the leeks from the bowl and shake out any excess water. If they still seem sandy, rinse under running water.

When the fowl is done, remove it from the stock, place it in a bowl, taking care to keep it whole, and let cool. When cool, cut the fowl into eighths, then cover with plastic wrap and refrigerate until serving. Strain the stock through a sieve. Reserve 10 cups of stock (you will need 6 cups for the Sauce Velouté and 4 cups for the rice).

Add the remaining stock to a large saucepan and bring to a boil. Add the leeks, carrots, cabbage, and turnips. Reduce the heat, and cook the vegetables at a high simmer until they are tender, about 30 minutes. When all the vegetables have cooked, turn off the heat, cover, and reserve.

MAKE THE SAUCE VELOUTÉ: Bring the stock to a boil. In a 2-quart saucepan, melt 4 tablespoons of the butter over low heat. Sir in the flour and cook, stirring constantly, until the flour begins to turn a light golden color, about 2 minutes. Remove the pan from the heat and let

SERVES 6

POULE AU POT

1 lemon

1 5 to 6 pound fowl, trussed

8 quarts water

2 pounds veal bones

1 onion, peeled and spiked with 6 whole cloves

1 whole head of garlic, cut in half crosswise

1 bay leaf, a few sprigs of thyme, and a handful of parsley

4 whole leeks

2 pounds carrots, peeled and cut into 4-inch lengths

1 cabbage, cut into eighths and each section tied like a package with kitchen string

2 pounds turnips, trimmed and peeled

SAUCE VELOUTÉ

6 cups chicken stock (from the poule au pot)

6 tablespoon unsalted butter, at room temperature

4 tablespoons flour

Sea salt and black pepper to taste

cool for 1 minute to allow the butter and flour to settle. Then begin adding the hot fowl stock, 1 cup at a time, whisking continuously until well incorporated. Continue whisking while bringing the sauce back to a boil. At this point, reduce the heat and simmer for 1 hour. Skim the top of the sauce occasionally, and stir it periodically to prevent the sauce from sticking or burning. The sauce is ready when it is thick enough to coat a spoon. Stir in the remaining 2 tablespoons butter a little at a time until well incorporated. Add salt and pepper to taste. If you are not using the sauce right away, cover with parchment paper until ready to use to prevent a film from forming on top of the sauce. Reheat in a double boiler.

To assemble and serve the poule au pot, bring the vegetables back to a boil in their broth. Place the cut fowl in the broth. Reduce heat and add salt and pepper to taste. When heated thoroughly, remove the fowl and vegetables from the broth and arrange on a platter. Serve with the Sauce Velouté and the rice. The remaining fowl broth is delicious and should be saved for another use. It can be refrigerated for 2 days or frozen for up 2 months.

JASMINE RICE WITH KAFFIR LIME LEAVES AND GARLIC

SERVES 6

4 cups chicken stock (from poule au pot, preceding recipe)
2 whole cloves garlic, peeled
3 kaffir lime leaves
1 teaspoon salt
2 cups jasmine rice

I adore the delicate citrus flavor of kaffir lime when cooked with rice. It's subtle infusion is a perfect compliment for the poule au pot.

In a 2-quart saucepan, bring the stock, garlic, kaffir lime leaves, and salt to a boil. Add the rice, stir, and return to a boil. Reduce the heat, cover, and simmer for 20 minutes. Turn off the heat and let the rice sit for 10 minutes. When ready to serve, transfer the rice to a serving dish and remove the lime leaves.

TARTE TATIN WITH CRÈME FRAÎCHE

MAKES ONE 9 1/2-INCH TART

DOUGH

1 1/4 cups all-purpose flour

1/4 teaspoon kosher salt

1 stick (4 ounces) unsalted butter,
cut into small pieces, chilled

2 to 3 tablespoons ice water

FILLING

3 tablespoons unsalted butter,
at room temperature

3/4 cup sugar

5 to 6 medium apples (Baldwin, Fuji, or
Mutsu), peeled, cored, and cut into quarters

1 cup crème fraîche, for serving

Requires 2 hours advance preparation

Tarte Tatin is one of my favorite desserts to make in the fall when the sugar content and texture of the apples is optimal.

I have made this tart many times and have found that using a copper tart tatin mold makes all the difference, as copper distributes and holds heat evenly (see Sources).

MAKE THE DOUGH: Sift the flour and salt together into a large bowl. Add the chilled butter. With your fingers, gently work the butter and flour together until the dough becomes crumbly. Add 2 tablespoons of ice water and, still using your hands, work together and shape into a ball. If the dough is still crumbly, add up to 1 tablespoon additional water. Place the ball of dough on a floured work surface, and gently pat it into a 5-inch round disk. Wrap the disk in plastic wrap and refrigerate for 2 hours. (The dough can be refrigerated for up to 2 days or frozen for up to 2 weeks.)

Roll out the dough on a floured work surface to 1/8-inch thickness. Cut the dough into an 11-inch round. Place the round on a parchment-lined baking sheet and refrigerate until ready to assemble the tart.

PREPARE THE FILLING: Spread the butter evenly over the inside, bottom, and sides of the tart pan. Pour the sugar into the pan and spread it evenly over the bottom. Starting at the outer edge of the pan, place the apple quarters, cut side down, into the pan, fitting them snuggly together until the pan is covered with the apples. If there are any left-over apples, add them after you begin the cooking and the apples begin to shrink.

Preheat the oven to 350 degrees. Place the tart pan over medium-high heat and cook the apples until the sugar begins to caramelize and turns an amber color, 25 to 30 minutes. At this point turn off the heat immediately. Gently press down on the apples with a wooden spoon to fill any empty spaces between them. Remove the dough round from the refrigerator and place it over the tart. Gently press the edges of the dough down around the apples inside the pan.

Place the tart in the preheated oven and bake for 30 minutes or until the pastry turns golden brown. Remove the tart from the oven and let it rest for 5 minutes. Place a serving plate at least 2 inches larger than the pan over the top of the tart. Gently shake the pan, invert the tart onto the plate, and remove the pan. If any apples have stuck to the pan, use a spatula to gently remove them and place back on the tart. Serve warm with crème fraîche.

If I could only eat first courses in Italy, I would

VEAL CARNE CRUDA

SAUTÉED PORCINI MUSHROOMS WITH GARLIC, PARSLEY, AND OLIVE OIL

GNUDI: SPINACH RAVIOLI TUSCAN STYLE

RAGU FAMILY STYLE

CANARINO TEA

Autumn is my favorite season in Italy. My favorite autumn dishes there, whether I have them in a restaurant or at a friend's house, are always first courses. In restaurants I want to order all of them, and when I'm a guest in someone's home, I pray for second helpings. What I've done here is create a menu of some of the most memorable first courses I've had in different regions of Italy.

VEAL CARNE CRUDA

Requires 1 hour advance preparation

I have had many great meals with winemaker Angelo Gaja in the Piedmont. One of the best was at a small trattoria in his village of Barbaresco where I could see the pasta cook rolling out sheets of dough and cutting the tagliatelle to order. Simplicity and perfection were joined in a way I have never forgotten. Every dish arrived with the minimum of garnish so that all the ingredients spoke eloquently for themselves. From my memory of this meal I have chosen a veal tartar which is both unusual and easy. It went well with Angelo's wines, of course, and I have made it many times since.

Place the garlic in the olive oil, cover, and let sit for 1 hour. Discard the garlic.

Put the ground veal in a bowl and stir in the garlic oil and lemon juice. Mix until well combined. Cover and refrigerate.

When ready to serve, remove the veal from the refrigerator. Add the salt and pepper and mix well.

Place ¼ cup of the veal mixture in the center of 4 serving plates. With a spatula, gently press down to a ½ inch thickness. Drizzle with some olive oil and season with more salt and pepper. Serve with the lemon wedges.

SERVES 4

2 cloves garlic, peeled, halved lengthwise, and crushed

¼ cup extra-virgin olive oil, plus more for drizzling

1 pound veal cutlets, coarsely ground

Freshly squeezed juice of 2 lemons, strained

1 teaspoon sea salt, plus more for seasoning

Freshly ground black pepper to taste

1 lemon, cut into 4 wedges

SAUTÉED PORCINI MUSHROOMS WITH GARLIC, PARSLEY, AND OLIVE OIL

What is more autumnal than porcini mushrooms with their woody, earthy, smoky taste? They can be good at other times of the year too, but their perfume is most distinctive in the fall. Also known as cèpes, porcinis are wonderful when dried and used to infuse a sauce. This preparation works well for other mushrooms if porcinis are not available.

Using a mushroom brush or a cloth, brush the mushrooms to remove any dirt or loose particles. Then wipe them off with a slightly damp cloth and slice them ¼-inch thick. Heat the olive oil in a 12-inch skillet over high heat. Add the mushrooms in one layer and cook until the bottom side of the mushrooms are brown, 1 to 2 minutes. Turn over and cook for 2 more minutes, shaking the pan so they don't stick.

Add the garlic, parsley, and wine and cook over high heat for an additional 2 minutes or until wine has almost evaporated Place on a serving dish and season with salt and pepper. Serve immediately.

SERVES 4

2 large porcini mushrooms (about 5 ounces total)

3 tablespoons extra-virgin olive oil

2 cloves garlic, peeled and coarsely chopped

¼ cup chopped fresh flat-leaf parsley leaves

2 to 3 tablespoons dry white wine

Sea salt and freshly ground black pepper to taste

GNUDI: SPINACH RAVIOLI TUSCAN STYLE

SERVES 4

Makes 12 raviolis.

TOMATO SAUCE

Makes 3 1/2 cups

3 tablespoons extra-virgin olive oil

1 small onion, peeled and diced

2 cloves garlic, peeled and crushed

1 carrot, peeled and grated (about 1/4 cup)

1 stalk celery with leaves, trimmed and diced (about 1/2 cup)

1 28-ounce can whole tomatoes, chopped, juices reserved (see Sources)

Sea salt and freshly ground black pepper to taste

RAVIOLI

1 pound fresh spinach leaves without stems

2 teaspoons sea salt

1 cup fresh sheep's milk ricotta cheese, finely chopped

2 whole eggs plus 1 egg white, lightly beaten

1/2 teaspoon freshly grated nutmeg

3/4 cup all-purpose flour, plus more for dusting

3 quarts water or stock

1/2 cup olive oil

1/2 cup fresh sage leaves (optional)

1/2 cup freshly grated Parmigiano

Requires 2 hours advance preparation

Some of my favorite chiantis come from the Castello Di Monsanto Winery owned by the Bianchi family. The Bianchis have a cellar of their wines that stretches back to the 1960s. Lunch is always exquisitely simple, and almost always several older vintages of wines are poured. From the many wonderful dishes I've eaten at Castello Di Monsanto, I've chosen this spinach ravioli because it is such an unusual regional dish. Not wrapped in pasta, the ravioli are more like dumplings or gnocchi than conventional ravioli. Naturally they are perfect with the Chianti Il Poggio from Monsanto!

The trick to making these dumplings is not to use too much flour and to use a very fresh ricotta (available at specialty cheese shops). Sheep's milk ricotta cheese is an excellent choice if you can find it because it is a bit dryer and firmer than whole milk ricotta. If you are using whole cow's milk ricotta, place it in a fine mesh sieve lined with cheesecloth and placed over a bowl for several hours to allow all the excess liquid to drain out. This recipe can be easily doubled.

MAKE THE TOMATO SAUCE: Heat the oil in a 4-quart saucepan over medium-high heat. Add the onion, garlic, carrot, and celery, and cook until lightly browned, for 2 to 3 minutes, stirring occasionally. Add the tomatoes and their juices and bring to a boil. Reduce the heat and simmer, partially covered, for 30 minutes, stirring frequently to prevent sticking. Season with salt and pepper. Remove from the heat and let cool. When cool, pour the tomato sauce into a blender and puree. Reheat before serving.

MAKE THE RAVIOLI: Soak the spinach leaves in a large bowl of cool water. Let stand for 1 hour. Drain the spinach in a colander. Place the spinach leaves in a steamer with boiling water, sprinkle with 1 teaspoon of the salt and steam for 10 minutes. Remove the spinach from the steamer and place in a colander. When cool enough to handle, gently squeeze out any excess water until the spinach is completely dry. Chop it very finely (you should have about 1 cup).

Place the spinach, ricotta cheese, eggs, nutmeg, and the remaining teaspoon salt in a large bowl and mix until thoroughly combined.

Add the flour to the spinach mixture and stir until it is incorporated. The dough should be a little sticky. Dust your hands with flour. Then, place a heaping tablespoonful of the dough into the palm of your hand and shape it into an oval ball, about 2- by- 1 1/2 inches. Place on a lightly floured baking sheet and repeat until all the spinach mix-

ture has been used. You should have 12 dumplings. Refrigerate the dumplings for 1 hour covered, or up to 4 hours.

In a large 8-quart stockpot, add the water and some salt and bring to a boil. In a small saucepan, heat the tomato sauce. (Once you begin to make the dumplings, everything should be ready to go, so you can serve them immediately.)

Heat the olive oil in a saucepan large enough to hold the sage leaves in a single layer over medium-high heat. Add the sage leaves and fry until the sage leaves turn a light brown color and become crisp, 1 to 2 minutes. Be careful not to burn the leaves. Remove the leaves from the oil with a slotted spoon and drain them on a plate covered with paper towels. Keep warm.

Add the dumplings to the boiling water. Poach for 8 to 10 minutes. When the dumplings rise to the top they are ready. Pour the heated tomato sauce into a shallow serving bowl and the raviolis on top. Sprinkle with the Parmigiano and fried sage. Serve immediately.

RAGU FAMILY STYLE

Requires 3 hour advance preparation

SERVES 6 TO 8

½ cup olive oil

1 medium onion, finely diced (about ¾ cup)

1 stalk celery with leaves, finely diced (about ¾ cup)

1 carrot, finely diced (about ¾ cup)

1 pound sirloin steak, coarsely ground

¼ pound pork loin, coarsely ground

1 ounce beef suet, finely diced

1 chicken neck

5 cups chicken stock

⅔ cup dry red wine, preferably a good Chianti

3 whole canned tomatoes (about ½ pound), coarsely chopped

1 slice of lemon peel, about 4 inches by ½ inch

1 cup whole milk

2 teaspoons sea salt, plus more for seasoning

½ teaspoon ground cinnamon

½ teaspoon freshly ground nutmeg

¼ teaspoon freshly ground allspice

Freshly ground black pepper to taste

½ cup heavy cream

Cooked tagliatelle, for serving

Ragus. I have had them all over Italy. I love them all, particularly when served with fresh tagliatelle. Since I never have the time to make pasta, I improvise by buying dried egg pastas (see Sources). When serving pasta with ragu, my formula is 3 ounces of fresh or dried tagliatelle per person. This recipe is inspired by several different versions of ragu Bolognese. I always double the recipe so I can freeze some to use later.

An Italian chef once told me that when you buy meat for a ragu you should have the butcher put it through the grinder only once as it will hold up better in the sauce. Use a pan that is wide and shallow enough for the ragu to cook evenly and for the moisture to evaporate.

Heat the olive oil in a 3-inch deep 6-quart sauté pan, 10 to 12 inches in diameter, over medium-low heat. Add the onion, celery, and carrot, and cook, stirring frequently, for 25 minutes or until the vegetables caramelize a bit and are golden brown. Add the ground meats, suet, and chicken neck, raise the heat to high, and cook the meats, stirring frequently, to insure even browning. (It is very important the meats brown well and become a little crusty. Don't worry if the pan becomes sticky.)

Meanwhile, pour the chicken stock into a saucepan and bring it to a simmer, set aside. Once the meats have browned, add the wine to the pan, bring to a boil and cook, stirring until almost all the wine has evaporated, about 1 minute. Stir in the tomatoes, lemon peel, and the warmed chicken stock, and return to a boil. Stir in the milk, salt, cinnamon, nutmeg, allspice, and pepper. Reduce the heat and simmer for 2 hours, partially covered, stirring every 20 to 30 minutes. Stir in the heavy cream after 1 hour of cooking.

When the ragu has cooked, discard the lemon peel and chicken neck. Season with salt and pepper . Serve the ragu with fresh-cooked tagliattele or dried egg tagliattele.

CANARINO TEA

SERVES 4

2 lemons

1 quart water

When I'm in Florence, a meal that does not end with with a pot of canarino tea is not complete for me. Named for the color of canaries, this tea is made with lemon peels only. Often I add herbs such as rosemary, but for purists it is all about the lemon peel.

Cut the peel from the lemons in strips from top to bottom as far from the flesh as possible. Place the peels in a teapot. Boil the water and pour over the lemon. Let steep for 5 minutes, then serve.

I have nothing to declare: a smuggler's feast

POILÂNE BREAD WITH IBERIAN HAM

FOIE GRAS TERRINE WITH QUINCE POACHED IN MONBAZILLAC

VACHERIN CHEESE WITH RATTE POTATOES

GRILLED MUSCOVY DUCK BREAST WITH FLAGEOLET BEANS

AGEN PRUNES AND ARMAGNAC

Can someone please explain why Velveeta cheese is legal in this country, but a raw milk Vacherin from France is contraband? Or why it's illegal to import a certain butter made with fresh cream and sea salt but we can live with margarine? I don't get it, but since it is illegal to import many of my favorite ingredients, I've often had to take matters into my own hands—or pockets as the case may be.

Once, when I was returning from Paris, where I had attended a huge food show, I had so many jams, salts, and mustards along with the supplies I usually sneak in (truffles, cheese, and wine), that even I knew I was pushing it. When the customs officer looked at all my luggage and asked, "Do you have anything to declare," I paused, and replied, "Well as a matter of fact I do. My dog Bessie is traveling with me. Would you like to see her papers?" I made it through with all my treasures intact.

When I travel I love to bring back an ingredient I've just discovered and re-create an experience from my trip to share with my friends. This menu is a smuggler's feast of memorable finds: Iberian ham from Spain, butter made with sea salt, Poilâne bread from Paris, raw milk cheeses from Barthelemy (a favorite cheese shop of mine in Paris), and so forth. A dinner like this is centered around a few special tastes accompanied by a great bottle of wine.

Of course, not all the food I bring back is contraband, but knowing that a few of the ingredients of a dinner risked being confiscated always gives the evening a certain excitement.

POILÂNE BREAD WITH IBERIAN HAM

SERVES 6

6 slices Poilâne pain levain

2 tablespoons unsalted butter, at room temperature

1 pound Iberian ham, thinly sliced, or Parma Proscuitto

Poilâne bread was one of the first things I smuggled home from Paris. This was at a time when very little good bread was being produced in the States. Now, not only can you get Poilâne bread in the States, but there are many fine bakeries (see Sources) across the country with exceptional products. What appeals to me about the Poilâne loaf is not just the subtle taste of the sourdough but its size. Sliced, it produces wonderful long pieces that are perfect for open-faced sandwiches.

Bellota and Bellota in Paris imports the finest Spanish Iberian ham. It is made from black pigs fed only on the acorns from hundred-year-old oak trees. It is certainly the best ham I have ever tasted. Similar in texture to Parma Proscuitto, it is sweet and in some cases you can taste the nuttiness from the acorns.

Toast the pain levain. Spread 1 teaspoon of unsalted sweet butter over the tops of each slice of bread. Place 2 to 3 slices of ham on the butter. Slice the bread into 6 slices. Serve immediately.

FOIE GRAS TERRINE WITH QUINCE POACHED IN MONBAZILLAC

SERVES 6

1 bottle (750 ml) Monbazillac or Sauternes

1 cup sugar

1 vanilla bean, split

1 cinnamon stick (about 3 inches)

2 quince (about ¾ pound each), peeled, cored, and cut into eighths

½ pound goose or duck liver foie gras terrine

12 slices pain de mie, lightly toasted

Coarse sea salt and coarsely ground black pepper

Monbazillac is a poor man's Sauternes. Though it is available in specialty wine stores across the country, I find the best selection is in Paris. I usually bring a bottle or two back with me, especially if I am also carrying back a foie gras terrine from Jean Legrand (see Sources).

Pain de mie is my choice of bread for Foie Gras. The best is from Poujauran in Paris. I always bring some back and keep it in my freezer for just this moment. Substitute any firm white bread.

In a large saucepan, add the Monbazillac, sugar, vanilla bean, and cinnamon stick and bring to a boil. Reduce the heat and simmer for 2 minutes or until the sugar has dissolved. Add the quince slices to the Monbazillac syrup, partially cover, and simmer until the quince are tender when pierced with a sharp knife, 25 to 30 minutes.

Using a slotted spoon, remove the quince slices and continue to cook the syrup at a high simmer for an additional 10 minutes. Discard the cinnamon stick. Scrape the seeds from the vanilla bean into the syrup and then discard the peel. Pour the syrup over the quince, cool, and refrigerate until ready to serve or up to 2 weeks.

To serve, place 2 pieces of quince on individual serving dishes along with a slice of foie gras and 2 slices of toasted pain de mie. Spoon a tablespoon of the quince syrup over the sliced quince. Serve the coarse sea salt and freshly ground pepper on the side.

VACHERIN CHEESE WITH RATTE POTATOES

There is no other seasonal cheese I enjoy as much as a raw milk Vacherin. It is in season from November to February. It is a creamy cow's milk cheese wrapped in a spruce band, which flavors the cheese. Vacherin can be spread on bread but I adore serving it with steamed ratte potatoes. A ratte potato is a French name for a small potato, similar to a fingerling. When cooked, they are sweet and the flesh is dry. They are available in specialty grocery stores or in farmers' markets around the country (see Sources). You can substitute any small potato.

Place a steamer basket in a 4-quart saucepan and fill with water just to the bottom of the steamer. Place the potatoes evenly on the basket. Sprinkle with 1 teaspoon of the sea salt. Bring the water to a boil, cover, and steam for 20 minutes.

Using tongs, remove the potatoes from the steamer basket and place in a bowl. Sprinkle with the remaining 1 teaspoon sea salt.

To serve, using a spoon or knife, carefully remove the the top layer of the vacherin cheese. Spoon some cheese onto an individual serving plate along with a few warm potatoes. Repeat with the remaining cheese and potatoes. Serve immediately.

SERVES 4

1 pound ratte potatoes, washed and scrubbed

2 teaspoons sea sea salt

1 1/2-pound wheel ripe Vacherin cheese

GRILLED MUSCOVY DUCK BREAST WITH FLAGEOLET BEANS

Requires 24 hours advance preparation

Flageolet beans are a French Kidney bean, pale green in color and most often used when dried (see Sources). Even though they are available in this country I always bring some back when I see them in farmer's markets in France. I buy them, for instance, at the wonderful Marche Biologique in Paris. Though I serve them here with Muscovy Duck breast, they are also a great side to lamb or salmon.

Depending on the age of your beans they might need to cook longer than specified here. Cook until the beans are tender, and add additional water if necessary—just enough to cover the beans.

Soak the beans overnight in 2 quarts cold water. Drain the beans and add to a large saucepan. Add the remaining 1 1/2 quarts cold water, the beans, bay leaf, garlic, thyme, and 1 teaspoon salt and bring to boil. Reduce the heat and simmer for 1/2 hour. Add the carrot and simmer, partially covered, for an additional 1 to 1 1/2 hours, until the beans are tender. Stir in the butter and season with salt and pepper.

Preheat the oven to 375 degrees. Wash the duck breast halves, then place fat side up on a chopping board. Using a sharp knife, slice

SERVES 4

1 cup dried flageolet beans

3 1/2 quarts cold water

1 bay leaf

2 cloves garlic, peeled and left whole

1 sprig fresh thyme

1 teaspoon sea salt, plus more for seasoning

1 carrot, peeled and finely diced

1 tablespoon unsalted butter

2 teaspoons sea salt

Freshly ground black pepper to taste

1 whole muscovy duck breast, cut in half

Paris Shopping List

Fouquet
2 jars Poivre aux Épices
Lavender + Orange Honey, lg jars
1 Box caramels assorted
2 jars sour cherries.

Denise Acabo
P/u more Bernachon Chocolate bars, Brésilien a must!!

Poujauran
2 Loaves Pain de Mie, sliced

Bellota & Bellota

2 pieces Jambon Ibériques
(P/u @ Rue Jean Nicot next to Poujauran)
2 jars Mêlée de Piments

Jean Leprard

2 ½ kilo pieces Foie Gras, packed for plane
2 jars Neiêe de Cèdre

Grimmens Market (3400 Raspail)
Het more Vanilla beans
Look for Fleur de Sel from Guérande

Ladurée

2 Boxes assorted macaroons. (small size)

Augé
1 Bottle Bas Armagnac 88' Domaine Boingnères
look for some Condrieu + Macon from Thevenet

6 $\frac{1}{8}$-inch incisions along the fat lengthwise then 3 slices crosswise. Season both sides of the duck breasts with salt and pepper. Heat a 12-inch skillet and place the duck fat side down in the pan. Cook for 5 minutes over medium heat. Turn over and cook for another 5 minutes. Remove the duck breasts from the pan and place them in a baking dish.

Bake the duck breasts in the preheated oven for 10 minutes for medium rare, 15 to 20 for medium. Remove from the oven and let the duck breasts rest for 5 minutes before slicing into $\frac{1}{4}$-inch diagonal slices.

To serve, spoon some flageolet beans onto a dinner plate, then arrange half the sliced duck on top. Season with salt and pepper. Repeat with the remaining beans and duck. Serve immediately.

AGEN PRUNES AND ARMAGNAC

MAKES 8 TO 10

1 cup cold water

$\frac{1}{2}$ cup sugar

1 pound Agen prunes, with pits

3 cups Bas Armagnac

Requires 24 hours advance preparation

It wasn't until I had a 100-year-old Armagnac that I understood the marriage of prunes and Armagnac. That had a subtle essence of prunes. In France, not only wine and cheese have designated appellations, fruit does also as in the case with the prunes from Agen. I believe these are the finest prunes produced—plump and moist (see Sources). Any other prunes can be substituted in this recipe of course.

In a large saucepan, combine the water and sugar and bring to a boil. Reduce the heat and stir until the sugar is dissolved, about 1 minute. Add the prunes and Armagnac. Bring to a boil and then simmer over medium-high heat for 2 minutes. Remove from the heat and let cool.

When the prunes are cool, transfer to a 1-quart glass jar or container. Pour the syrup over the prunes. Make sure the syrup covers the prunes in the jar. If not, add a little more Armagnac to cover. Let cool completely, cover, and refrigerate for 24 hours before serving.

To serve, return the prunes to room temperature and divide among small serving bowls along with some of the syrup. (The prunes can be stored for up to 2 months in the refrigerator.)

Easy, just give me easy

HALIBUT FILLET BAKED IN PARCHMENT WITH SALSA VERDE
FINGERLING POTATOES STEAMED ON A BED OF THYME, THEN RE-FRIED
ROQUEFORT CHEESE WITH LAVENDER HONEY

Whenever friends ask me for a recipe or a menu, they usually begin by saying, "I just want something easy. I'm not a great cook like you, so what should I make?" By now I understand that everyone wants to cook an impressive meal and yet they want it to be easy to put together. Well, most dishes are simple; what's challenging for many people is not knowing which dishes can be made ahead of time. I always do as much of the prep as I can before people arrive. That way I'm relaxed, everyone else is relaxed, and the meal looks effortless. In the case of this meal, an easy salsa verde can be done ahead of time and it dresses up a simple fish.

For dessert I love the combination of a salty Roquefort cheese and sweet lavender honey—nothing could be simpler. This menu follows the formula of great ingredients, easy combinations, and simple preparation that ends up impressing everyone.

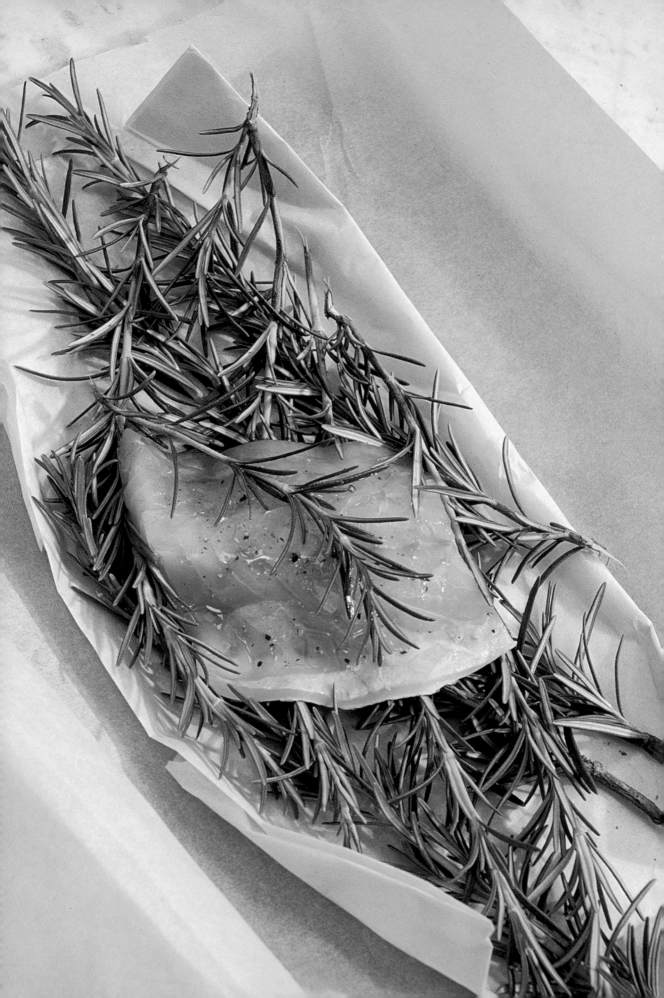

HALIBUT FILLET BAKED IN PARCHMENT WITH SALSA VERDE

Halibut is a firm, white-fleshed fish. If undercooked it is tough and chewy and if overcooked can be very dry. I have found that cooking it in parchment is foolproof. Most fishmongers cut halibut steaks, but I prefer a fillet because it is more flaky when cooked. If halibut is not available substitute striped bass or cod. When using parchment paper select unbleached, which is free of chemicals.

MAKE THE SALSA VERDE: Slice the crusts off the bread and discard. Place the bread on a small plate and drizzle both sides with the red wine vinegar.

Soak the anchovies in a bowl of cold water for 30 minutes. Remove the bones and reserve the fillets.

In a marble mortar, combine the anchovies, garlic, and capers. Pound the mixture into a paste. Add the bread and parsley and pound to a fine paste. Slowly pour in the olive oil, stirring constantly until all the oil is incorporated. Add salt to taste, if necessary.

PREPARE THE HALIBUT: Preheat the oven to 360 degrees. Cut 4 sheets of parchment paper into 6 12-inch squares on a work surface. Place two sprigs of rosemary in the center of each piece of parchment, then place a halibut fillet on top of the rosemary sprigs. Drizzle with a little olive oil. Bring the front and back of each piece of parchment together over the centers of each fillet. Gently fold together 3 times and then fold the ends of the paper under the packets. Place the packets in a heavy-duty baking pan and bake for 25 minutes. Remove the fish from the oven and let it rest for 5 minutes before serving.

To serve, unfold the parchment papers and gently slide a spatula under the fillets, lifting each one onto an individual serving plate. Spoon several tablespoons of salsa verde on top.

SERVES 6

SALSA VERDE

1 slice ½-inch-thick hearty white bread, about 4 inches by 2 inches

1 tablespoon red wine vinegar

2 anchovy fillets, packed in salt

2 cloves garlic, peeled

2 tablespoons capers in brine or vinegar, drained and rinsed

1 cup loosely packed flat-leaf parsley leaves, washed and dried

1 cup extra-virgin olive oil

Sea salt, to taste

HALIBUT

12 3-inch sprigs fresh rosemary

6 halibut fillets, ½ pound each

Olive oil

FINGERLING POTATOES STEAMED ON A BED OF THYME, THEN RE-FRIED

SERVES 4

1 bunch fresh thyme (about 1 ounce)
1 pound fingerling potatoes
2 teaspoons sea salt, plus more for seasoning
¼ cup olive oil
Freshly ground black pepper to taste

Fingerling potatoes are long white potatoes shaped like fingers, whose cooked flesh is firm and dry. If you can't find fingerling potatoes you can substitute small Yukon gold potatoes or small creamer potatoes.

In a steamer large enough to hold the potatoes in one layer, line the basket with the thyme. Wash the potatoes and place them on the thyme. Sprinkle with the 2 teaspoons sea salt and steam until tender when pierced with a sharp knife, about 20 minutes. Remove from the steamer and place on a plate to cool.

Place a piece of parchment or plastic wrap on a cutting board. When the potatoes are cool enough to handle, lay them out 2 inches apart on the paper. Place another piece of parchment paper or plastic wrap over the potatoes. Using a meat pounder or a heavy skillet, gently flatten the potatoes until they are ¼-inch thick.

Heat a 12-inch skillet over high heat and add 2 tablespoons of the olive oil. Add half the potatoes and cook until golden brown, 2 to 3 minutes per side. Repeat with the remaining olive oil and potatoes. Place on a platter and sprinkle with sea salt and pepper. Sprinkle some of the thyme leaves from the steamer over the potatoes. Serve warm.

ROQUEFORT CHEESE WITH LAVENDER HONEY

SERVES 6

½ pound Roquefort cheese
6 tablespoons lavender honey, room temperature

The French say that a little bit of cheese after your meal satisfies your sweet tooth. I agree—but it doesn't hurt to add something sweet! I have always been a big fan of combining honey with sheep's milk cheeses. Lavender honey is wonderful with one of the most famous sheep's milk cheeses, Roquefort. The sweet and salty combination is just sublime.

Cut the wedge of Roquefort into 6 slices. Place 1 slice on each of six individual serving plates. Drizzle each slice with 1 tablespoon lavender honey.

From Bombay to Brooklyn for Thanksgiving

ROASTED TURKEY WITH TANDOORI SPICES

ROASTED HUBBARD SQUASH WEDGES WITH GARAM MASALA

BASMATI RICE WITH SAFFRON AND CLOVES

RED LENTILS WITH TAMARIND AND DATES

POTATOES WITH TOMATO CURRY

CREAMED SPINACH WITH CARDAMOM AND SHIITAKE MUSHROOM DUXELLE

STEAMED BRUSSELS SPROUTS WITH GHEE AND SEA SALT

CRANBERRY AND GINGER CHUTNEY

MINT AND CHILE RAITA

CLOVER ROLLS WITH ROSEMARY

PUMPKIN AND ARBORIO RICE PUDDING

SHRIKAND (A CREAMY YOGURT DESSERT) WITH FRESH POMEGRANATE SEEDS

One Thanksgiving, while going by taxi from Manhattan to Brooklyn for dinner, my friend Mona asked the driver, who happened to be Indian, what he was doing for the holiday. He proudly replied that he was going to fire up the tandoori oven in his backyard and make a tandoori turkey. When Mona told me this story, I was immediately taken with the driver's idea and eventually came up with this menu, Thanksgiving with a touch of India.

When I was in India, I had my first real Indian Bhandara, a humble but elaborate feast with many different dishes of contrasting flavors—salty, sour, bitter, hot, and sweet. What struck me about Mona's story was that Thanksgiving has a lot in common with the Bhandara. Now, I don't expect anyone to run out and buy a tandoori oven or even to cook this whole menu for Thanksgiving. You can just take the parts of it that appeal to you and make them along with your favorite traditional dishes. Whatever our background and whatever our menu, we can all gather to share a blessing and express our gratitude for the things we have been given.

ROASTED TURKEY WITH TANDOORI SPICES

16 hours advance preparation (optional)

MAKES ONE 20 TO 25 POUND TURKEY

1 20 to 25 pound fresh organic turkey (see Sources), rinsed and patted dry

WET BRINE

2 gallons water

11 1/2 cups kosher salt

1 1/2 cups sugar

2 whole heads of garlic, smashed

10 fresh bay leaves

2 tablespoons whole cloves

DRY RUB

2 tablespoons olive oil

2 tablespoons tandoori masala powder

1 tablespoon ground turmeric

2 teaspoons cayenne pepper

2 teaspoons sea salt

TURKEY AND VEGETABLES

2 sticks (1/2 pound) unsalted butter, melted

2 cups dry white wine

1 onion, peeled and sliced crosswise 1/4-inch thick

1 lemon, cut into eighths

1 cup cilantro leaves, washed and torn in pieces

At first I struggled with the idea of tandoori turkey because in a traditional tandoori you skin the fowl and cut it up before marinating it. Somehow the idea of turkey pieces presented on a platter at Thanksgiving just wouldn't do. I don't mind the bird being a shade on the orange side, but it has to be whole (see Sources). So I improvised with some traditional tandoori spices and roasted the turkey in one piece. The result was a turkey that still had the classic taste, just with livelier spicing. If I have the time I also like to marinate the turkey in a brine to tenderize it. This step is optional.

PREPARE THE WET BRINE: Bring the water to a boil and add the salt, sugar, garlic cloves, bay leaves, and cloves, and stir until the sugar is dissolved. Remove from the heat and let cool. Then refrigerate until chilled. Place the whole turkey into a 5-gallon nonreactive bucket. Pour the cold brine over the turkey and cover. Refrigerate for 12 hours.

PREPARE THE DRY RUB: Mix all the ingredients in a small bowl. Remove the turkey from the brine, drain in the kitchen sink, and pat dry. Place the turkey on a large platter and coat the turkey inside and out with the dry rub. Cover and refrigerate for 4 hours.

PREPARE THE TURKEY AND VEGETABLES: Preheat the oven to 350 degrees. Remove the turkey from the refrigerator and place breast side up on a rack in a deep roasting pan. Cover the turkey with a double layer of cheesecloth, 24 by 18 inches. Brush the cheesecloth with the melted butter. Cover the turkey with parchment paper then foil. Pour the wine into the pan and place in the oven. Bake the turkey for 4 hours, basting every hour. Remove the foil and paper and continue baking for 1 hour longer or until a thermometer registers 170 degrees when placed in the deepest part of thigh. Remove the turkey from the oven and let rest for 30 minutes.

Place the sliced onions, lemon wedges, and cilantro in a bowl. Mix together, then spread out onto a serving platter. Place the turkey onto the platter and serve.

ROASTED HUBBARD SQUASH WEDGES WITH GARAM MASALA

SERVES 10

1 tablespoon garam masala

1 tablespoon sugar

1 teaspoon sea salt

1 5-pound hubbard squash, sliced length-wise into tenths, seeds removed

2 tablespoons melted butter

This is a very simple way to prepare hubbard squash (you can substitute butternut squash). Garam masala is a Northern Indian blend of spices. Garam is Indian for warm. Masala is a term for spice blend. It is available in Indian or Middle Eastern specialty stores.

Preheat the oven to 350 degrees. In a small bowl, combine the garam masala, sugar, and salt, and reserve.

Brush the squash slices with the melted butter and spread evenly on a parchment-lined baking sheet. Sprinkle half of the spice mixture evenly on top. Place the squash in the oven and bake for 45 minutes. Remove the squash from the oven and sprinkle both sides of the squash slices with the remaining garam masala mixture. Place back in the oven and bake for an additional 15 minutes or until the squash is tender and golden brown. Serve immediately.

BASMATI RICE WITH SAFFRON AND CLOVES

SERVES 10 TO 12

4 cups water

2 teaspoons saffron threads

6 whole cloves

2 teaspoons sea salt

2 cups basmati rice, washed and drained

2 tablespoons unsalted butter, cut into small pieces

In a heavy pot bring the water, saffron, cloves, and salt to a boil. Stir in the rice and return to a boil. Reduce the heat, cover, and simmer for 20 minutes. Turn off the heat, and scatter the butter over the rice. Cover the pot and let the rice rest for 10 minutes. Fluff with a fork, remove cloves, and serve.

RED LENTILS WITH TAMARIND AND DATES

If space on the stove is a problem, this recipe can be made a day in advance and reheated just before serving. For some of the seasonings used here (tamarind, black mustard seeds, and curry leaves) see Sources.

In a large saucepan, bring the water and lentils to a boil. Reduce the heat, and simmer, partially covered, for 20 minutes. Then add the tamarind paste, dates, chiles, turmeric, and salt, and continue cooking over low heat for 10 minutes, stirring occasionally.

In a small skillet, heat the oil over medium-high heat. Add the black mustard seeds, and as soon as they begin to crackle, add the cumin seeds and curry leaves. Reduce the heat to low and cook for 1 minute, stirring occasionally, being careful not to burn anything. Remove the pan from the heat and stir the spices into the lentils. When ready to serve, reheat if necessary, and garnish with the cilantro.

SERVES 10 TO 12

3 cups water

1 cup split red lentils, washed

*3 ounces tamarind paste
(about 3 tablespoons)*

4 dried dates, pits removed and coarsely chopped

2 serrano chiles, cut in half lengthwise, seeds and ribs removed

3/4 teaspoon ground turmeric

1 teaspoon sea salt

2 tablespoons olive oil

1 teaspoon black mustard seeds

1 teaspoon whole cumin seeds

12 curry leaves

1 tablespoon cilantro leaves, washed and coarsely chopped

POTATOES WITH TOMATO CURRY

When using tomatoes out of season, I use the canned Organic Muir Glen brand. The quality is great, and they are available in most supermarkets across the country.

In a medium skillet, melt 1 tablespoon of the butter in the olive oil. Add the onion and cook over low heat until the onions are soft and transparent, about 5 minutes. Stir in the cumin seeds, curry powder, turmeric, and cayenne pepper. Then stir in the tomatoes, chicken stock, and 1 teaspoon salt, and cook over medium-high heat for 10 minutes, stirring occasionally. Add the cream and cook, stirring, for another 5 minutes. Remove from the heat and let cool. When the sauce is cool, pour it into a blender and puree until smooth, reserve.

Bring water to a boil in a large steamer. Add the potatoes, sprinkle with the remaining 1 teaspoon salt, cover, and steam until the potatoes are tender when pierced with a sharp knife 10 to 15 minutes. Remove from the heat.

Place the sauce in a large saucepan and bring to a high simmer. Add the remaining 2 tablespoons butter. Toss the potatoes in the sauce until they are completely coated. Serve immediately.

SERVES 10 TO 12

3 tablespoons unsalted butter

2 tablespoons olive oil

1 medium onion, peeled and finely diced

1 teaspoon whole cumin seeds

1 teaspoon curry powder

1/4 teaspoon turmeric

1/2 teaspoon cayenne pepper

1 cup canned diced tomatoes

1/2 cup chicken stock

2 teaspoons sea salt

1/2 cup heavy cream

2 pounds small Yukon gold potatoes (2 to 3 ounces each), peeled and cut in half crosswise

CREAMED SPINACH WITH CARDAMOM AND SHIITAKE MUSHROOM DUXELLE

Requires 1 hour advance preparation

SERVES 10 TO 12

Makes 3 quarts

*12 bunches fresh spinach, stems removed
(about 6 pounds)*

*2 sticks (1/2 pound) plus 1 tablespoon
unsalted butter*

1/2 cup diced shallots

*1 1/2 pounds shiitake mushrooms, stems
removed, finely diced*

1 tablespoon cardamom seeds, finely ground

2 teaspoons sea salt

Freshly ground black pepper

1 quart heavy cream

1 tablespoon plain bread crumbs

2 eggs, at room temperature

This recipe uses fresh spinach. You can substitute frozen but the texture and taste will be far less interesting. To get the grit out of fresh spinach I fill my sink with water and soak the spinach for at least an hour, turning and tossing it several times. If the spinach is really sandy sometimes I change the water once and repeat this process. You can wash and steam the spinach a day before.

Most Indian or Middle Eastern specialty grocery stores sell whole cardamom seeds without the pod. I grind the seeds in a coffee grinder. To clean out the grinder, I fill it with stale bread and grind it to a fine powder, then I toss the bread and wipe out the grinder. This process leaves no trace of flavors, even though a touch of cardamom in your coffee is actually quite good.

Soak the spinach leaves in a very large tub of water or in a clean sink for 1 hour. Plunge and stir the spinach leaves every 20 minutes. After an hour, if the spinach appears to be clean lift some of the leaves out of the water and place them in a colander, shaking to remove the excess water. Then transfer the leaves to a large bowl. Continue with the remaining spinach.

In a large steamer or skillet, steam the spinach until just wilted, 2 to 3 minutes. Remove from the steamer and cool (you may need to do this in several batches). When the spinach is cool enough to handle, place it in a mesh colander and press with your hands to get rid of any excess water. (This step can be done a day ahead. Leave the spinach in a colander inside a bowl, cover and refrigerate.) Chop the spinach and reserve.

Melt 2 sticks of the butter in a large skillet. Add the shallots and cook until transparent, about 1 minute. Add the mushrooms, cardamom, salt, and pepper to taste. Increase the heat to medium-high and cook for 5 minutes, stirring occasionally. Add the cream and bring to a boil. Reduce the heat and simmer for 10 minutes, stirring occasionally.

Preheat the oven to 350 degrees. Coat a baking dish with the remaining 1 tablespoon butter, then dust with the breadcrumbs.

Pour the spinach mixture into a large mixing bowl. Season with salt and pepper. Beat the eggs into the spinach mixture. Pour the spinach into the prepared baking dish, cover, and bake in the preheated oven for 30 minutes, or until firm when touched. Serve immediately.

STEAMED BRUSSELS SPROUTS WITH GHEE AND SEA SALT

Ghee is simply a butter that has been clarified and then simmered until all the moisture evaporates and the butter browns slightly. It takes on a subtle nutty flavor which makes it a nice complement to the brussels sprouts. Ghee is available in Indian specialty stores.

Remove the outer leaves and trim off the end of each sprout. Rinse well. Cut a small shallow "X" across the base of each sprout with a small knife.

In a steamer over boiling water, add the Brussels sprouts and cook, covered, until tender when pierced with a knife at the base of the stem, 10 to 12 minutes. Place the Brussels sprouts in a serving bowl and toss with the sea salt and ghee. Serve immediately.

SERVES 10 TO 12

2 pounds Brussels sprouts

2 teaspoons coarse sea salt

3 tablespoons ghee, warmed

CRANBERRY AND GINGER CHUTNEY

In a saucepan, combine the brown sugar, granulated sugar, water, candied ginger, tangerine juice, cider vinegar, fresh ginger and cinnamon. Bring to a boil, then reduce heat, partially cover, and simmer for 10 minutes, stirring often. Add the cranberries, return to a boil, then reduce the heat and simmer for 5 minutes. Remove from the heat and let cool. Remove the cinnamon stick and refrigerate until ready to serve. Then bring to room temperature before serving.

MAKES 1½ QUARTS

2 cups firmly packed brown sugar

1 cup granulated sugar

1½ cups water

1 cup candied ginger, cut into ⅛-inch cubes

1½ cups freshly squeezed tangerine juice

¼ cup cider vinegar

5 tablespoons grated fresh ginger

1 cinnamon stick (about 4 inches long)

2½ pounds fresh cranberries (about 12 cups)

MINT AND CHILE RAITA

This is a wonderful sauce to have with the tandoori turkey and all the sides in this menu. If you prefer a more classic gravy, you can serve the velouté sauce from the "Flight of Wines Menu," page 107, replacing the chicken stock in the recipe with turkey stock.

Be careful whenever you work with fresh chiles, because the chili oil can burn can burn your eyes and sensitive areas of your skin.

Place all of the ingredients in a small bowl. Stir until well-blended, cover, and refrigerate for 4 hours. Remove ½ hour before serving.

MAKES 1 CUP

1 cup whole milk yogurt

½ cup fresh mint leaves, washed and finely chopped

2 serrano chiles, seeds discarded, finely diced

Freshly squeezed juice of 1 lemon

½ teaspoon sea salt

CLOVER ROLLS WITH ROSEMARY

MAKES 1 DOZEN

1 1/4-ounce envelope active dry yeast

1/4 cup warm water (115 degrees)

1 tablespoon sugar

1 cup milk

6 tablespoons unsalted butter

1 1/2 teaspoons sea salt

1 egg, lightly beaten

4 to 4 1/4 cups all-purpose flour

2 teaspoons vegetable oil

12 1/2-inch sprigs rosemary

Requires 2 hours advance preparation

Even though this menu is Indian inspired, I must have a classic American dinner roll with my Thanksgiving meal. And even though this is an American roll, I find that it works perfectly well with this menu. This recipe can be easily doubled.

In a large bowl, stir together the yeast, warm water, and sugar, and let sit in a warm draft-free spot for 10 minutes.

In a small saucepan, combine the milk, 1 tablespoon of the butter, and the salt, and cook over medium-high heat, stirring constantly, until all the butter is melted. Turn off heat.

Using a wooden spoon gently stir the warm milk mixture and the egg into the yeast. Gradually add the flour until the dough is moist but not sticky. Transfer the dough onto a floured work surface and knead by hand until the dough is smooth and elastic, 8 to 10 minutes.

Transfer the dough to an oiled bowl, and turn over once to completely coat the dough with the oil. Cover the dough with plastic wrap and place in a warm spot until doubled in volume, about 1 hour and 15 minutes.

Butter a baking sheet and a muffin tin. Melt the remaining 5 tablespoons butter. Punch the dough down and divide into 3 balls weighing approximately 9 ounces each. Roll each each ball into a 12-inch log. Cut each log into 12 pieces and roll out pieces into balls. Place the balls on the baking sheet. Lightly baste each ball with some of the melted butter. Roll each ball in your hand so they are coated in butter. Place 3 balls into each muffin cup. Place each sprig of rosemary in the center of the muffins. Cover with plastic wrap and let rise until double in volume, about 45 minutes.

Preheat the oven to 400 degrees. After the rolls have doubled in volume, brush the tops with any remaining melted butter and bake for about 15 minutes or until they are golden brown. Serve warm. (The rolls can be frozen and warmed before serving.)

PUMPKIN AND ARBORIO RICE PUDDING

Requires 2 hours advance preparation

This dessert is a nice change from pumpkin pie. Because your oven will be empty, you can bake this at the last minute and serve it warm right out of the gratin dish. I like to serve it with fresh whipped cream. Why not? It's Thanksgiving and we have gone this far!

Preheat the oven to 370 degrees. Butter a 3-quart baking dish with sides at least 2 inches high. Set aside.

In a large saucepan, bring the water to a boil. Add the rice, reduce the heat, and simmer for 2 minutes. Drain the rice in a colander, rinse with cold water, and shake out all the excess water. When the rice is cool, spread it over the bottom of the prepared dish.

In a large saucepan, whisk together the milk, cream, pumpkin puree, sugar, cardamom, nutmeg, and sea salt. Bring the mixture almost to a boil. Pour the milk mixture carefully over the rice. Place the pudding in the preheated oven and bake for 10 minutes. Reduce the temperature to 325 degrees and continue baking for 2 hours. Let rest for 15 minutes before serving. Serve with the whipped cream.

SERVES 10 TO 12

Unsalted butter, for greasing
2 quarts water
1 cup arborio rice
3 cups whole milk
3 cups light or heavy cream
1 15-ounce can pumpkin puree or 1 3/4 cups fresh pumpkin puree
3/4 cup sugar
1 1/2 teaspoons freshly ground cardamom
1/2 teaspoon ground nutmeg
1 teaspoon sea salt
Whipped cream, see page 55

SHRIKAND (A CREAMY YOGURT DESSERT) WITH FRESH POMEGRANATE SEEDS

Requires 12 hours advance preparation

Shrikand is a yogurt dessert that I find very refreshing after such a rich meal. A tablespoon or two will do, because it is so filling. I use Persian saffron for this dessert when I can find it because the quality is exceptional (see Sources).

Line a mesh sieve with a double layer of cheesecloth. Place the sieve over a large, deep bowl. Put the yogurt in the sieve. The drained liquid should not touch the yogurt. Refrigerate overnight.

In a small nonreactive bowl, combine the cream and saffron. Cover and leave refrigerated overnight.

Remove the yogurt from the cheesecloth and place it in a bowl (you should have approximately 3 cups). Add the saffron-cream mixture, the sugar, and the cardamom. Stir well, cover, and refrigerate for 1 hour, or up to 24 hours, before serving. Stir again and transfer the shrikand to a serving bowl. Sprinkle the pomegranate seeds over the top and serve.

SERVES 8

5 cups whole milk yogurt
2 tablespoons heavy cream
1 teaspoon saffron threads
1 cup superfine sugar
1 teaspoon freshly ground cardamom seeds
Seeds from 1 pomegranate (about 1 cup)

HOW TO PLAY MAY I?

INGREDIENTS
Two decks of cards - well shuffled
4 to 6 players. 7 players is possible but not so good
A box of Bendix bitter mints

OBJECTIVE
To place the required number of runs and/or sets face up on the table and discard the remaining cards held in your hand. The Person who does this first is out and everyone else counts up the value of the cards remaining in their hands. This is their score. The person with the lowest score at the end of five rounds is the winner.

CARD VALUES WHICH MAKE UP THE SCORE AT THE END OF EACH ROUND
Ace and 2 of clubs are 15
King, Queen and Jack are 10
Everything else is its face value

TO GET RID OF CARDS YOU MAKE
Runs:These are three or more cards of the same suit in consecutive order.You can put down 6,7,8 of clubs and ace king queen of hearts. This would make two runs. The ace can only run with a king queen and below or run with two three and above. You cannot make a run consisting of a 2 then an Ace,then a King.
Sets: These are three or more cards of the same value, say all kings or all eights. In theory you could have a set of 8 cards.As a help there are two 2 of clubs in the two decks - these are wild and can represent any card you need.The other 2s are normal.

EACH ROUND IS DIFFERENT
In each round the players collect a combination of runs and sets.

Round 1	2 Sets
Round 2	1 Run and 1 Set
Round 3	2 Runs
Round 4	2 Sets and1Run
Round 5	2 Runs and 1 Set

STARTING
At the beginning of each of the five rounds one person shuffles and cuts to the person on their left. They deal 7 cards to each player and place the remaining cards face down on the table. This is the stock pile.

THE PLAY
When everyone is ready the person to the left of the dealer turns the top card from the stock pile and places it face up to start a discard pile. It is important that this turned card is visible to all players as soon as it is placed on the table. I find almost throwing the card down works well. It is now the go of the person to the left of the turner. The card turned is theirs.They can take this face up card or the unseen card from the top of the stock pile and try to get it to fit into a run or a set. However, when the card is turned all the other players may appeal 'May I!' which means they want that card. The person who's go it is may choose to let the person they consider said 'May I!' first, have the card.The person who wins the 'May I!' picks up first the top card of the stock pile and second the face up card they asked for. They now have two extra cards in their hand. The person who's go it is then picks up the concealed top card from the stock pile. Of course the person having the go may reply 'You may'nt' but of course they must then only take the turned up card. To finish their go,they put down a card on the discard pile in the same manner as the turner previously and at this point it is the go of the person to their left.

  The procedure in the above paragraph is repeated in a clockwise direction throughout the game. Once the person having the go has touched the card they are going to pick up it is too late for anyone to say 'May I!' I also say that if someone says 'May I!' by mistake and they are given permission to take the upturned card they must do so - they cannot change their mind....

PLACING RUNS AND SEQUENCES ON THE TABLE
On a players go, after they have picked up a card, they can put down their runs and/or sets on the table for all to see. They put down exactly the required amount: no more, no less. And, importantly, have one card over to put on the discard pile. They are then out. Usually there is more than one card to get rid of. Once a player has placed the sets and runs down on the table they can add their remaining cards to runs and sets already put down by other players. You cannot add to other people's sets and runs until you have placed down your own.

THE FIFTH ROUND IS THE CRUNCHER.
In the first four rounds you get your sets and runs down and spend the rest of the game reducing the value of your hand and discarding cards onto other people's sets and runs until one of you go out. You may or may not be first out but can be happy with a low score.In the fifth round you must go down and out in one go which leaves everyone else with a fist full of cards and a lot of points on their scores. So, to go down you must have 2 runs and 1 set plus one card to put on the discard pile. Usually the winner of this round is the winner of the game - but not always...

May I? Yes you may

ONION SOUP WITH COGNAC

WARM GRUYÈRE SANDWICH WITH MUSTARD AND FINES HERBES

BLOOD ORANGE GRANITA WITH VANILLA ICE CREAM

My dear friends Tessa Traeger and Patrick Kinmonth introduced me to the card game "May I?" I love card games, and this one is a favorite for an old-fashioned evening at home with friends. "May I" is so like life: Winning isn't everything and surprising reversals of fortune abound: You can win the first four rounds, lose the fifth, and lose the game or vice versa. You never know.

When it comes to food to go with an evening of cards, I want a simple meal—a great soup and sandwich. It's so nice just to sit down for the game without having spent hours in the kitchen. Onion soup is a good choice for a late-night supper like this one because it is substantial but not too filling. Although I'm not fond of the soggy bread and tough layer of cheese that overpower most traditional onion soups, I like to have melted Gruyère on hearty bread on the side. Doing so gives you the best of both worlds.

And, by the way, I like to have Bendick's Bittermints and some Cognac as the game reaches the wee small hours.

ONION SOUP WITH COGNAC

SERVES 6

BEEF STOCK

5 pounds beef bones

5 carrots, peeled and sliced into 2-inch lengths (about 4 cups)

5 stalks celery, sliced into 2-inch lengths (about 4 cups)

2 onions, peeled and quartered

1 head of garlic, halved crosswise

8 quarts cold water

2 bay leaves

1 teaspoon black peppercorns

6 stems parsley

ONION SOUP

4 tablespoons unsalted butter

1 pound yellow onions, peeled, and thinly sliced crosswise

1 clove garlic, peeled and smashed

1 4-inch cinnamon stick

1 teaspoon sea salt, plus more for seasonings

Freshly ground black pepper to taste

¼ cup Cognac

Requires 3 hours advance preparation if making your own stock

Making stock takes so much time that when I do it, I always make extra and freeze what I don't use. This soup works just as well when made with water, but is a bit less rich.

MAKE THE STOCK: Preheat the oven to 425 degrees. Place the bones, carrots, celery, onions, and garlic in a roasting pan. Place the pan in the preheated oven and roast for 30 minutes. Remove from the oven and place the roasted ingredients in a 10-quart stockpot. Add the water, bay leaves, peppercorns, and parsley and bring to a boil. Reduce the heat and cook at a high simmer, partially covered, for 3 hours. Skim as needed. Add cold water if necessary to make sure the ingredients are always covered with water.

Strain the stock through a fine sieve and reserve 3 quarts for the soup. (The stock keeps for 2 to 3 days in the refrigerator. The remaining 1 quart of stock can be frozen for up to 2 months.)

MAKE THE ONION SOUP: Melt the butter in a large saucepan over medium-high heat. Add the onions and garlic and cook over low heat, stirring frequently, until the onions become golden brown, 15 to 20 minutes.

Add the cinnamon stick, 1 teaspoon salt, and 3 quarts of the beef stock, and bring almost to a boil. Reduce the heat and simmer for 1 hour. Skim the soup from time to time. (The soup can be made ahead up to this point and refrigerated for up to 3 days.)

When ready to serve, bring the soup to a simmer over high heat and season with salt and pepper. Reduce the heat as soon as the soup reaches a boil and stir in the Cognac. Simmer for 2 minutes. Discard the cinnamon stick and serve immediately.

WARM GRUYÈRE SANDWICH WITH MUSTARD AND FINES HERBES

This recipe varies depending on the size of your bread. I prefer using large slices, up to 10 inches long and 4 inches wide. If you use smaller slices, use 12. I use a hearty rustic bread like pain levain or a sourdough rye (see Sources).

Preheat the broiler. Place the bread slices on a baking sheet and toast one side under the broiler until golden brown. Remove from the oven and turn the slices over. Brush the melted butter on each untoasted side. Then spread with mustard and sprinkle with the thyme leaves. Sprinkle the cheese evenly over the bread. Sprinkle with salt. Broil until the edges of the bread are golden brown and the cheese is melted, about 1 minute. Remove the bread slices from the oven, and place them on a cutting board. If using long slices of bread, cut into 3 to 6 pieces each, depending on the size of your bread. Place the sandwiches on a serving platter, and serve immediately.

SERVES 6

6 ¹/₂-inch-thick slices pain levain or sourdough bread, 10 inches by 4 inches (about 3 ounces each)
2 tablespoons unsalted butter, melted
Good-quality French mustard
1 tablespoon fresh thyme leaves
¹/₂ pound Gruyère cheese, grated
Sea salt

BLOOD ORANGE GRANITA WITH VANILLA ICE CREAM

Requires 2 hours advance preparation

Blood oranges are in season in autumn, and I love to use them to make a granita. They're a beautiful deep crimson red color, and they have both a sweet and tart orange flavor. This granita is great on its own, but is even more wonderful served with vanilla ice cream. The combination is reminiscent of a creamsicle.

Place the sugar and 1 cup of the blood orange juice in a saucepan. Bring the mixture almost to a boil, reduce the heat, and simmer for 1 minute or until the sugar is dissolved. Remove from the heat. Pour the orange syrup into a large metal bowl and stir in the remaining blood orange juice and the orange zest.

Place the bowl in the freezer. Every 2 hours stir the mixture with a fork and scrap down the sides of the bowl. Continue this process until the granita is completely frozen. Scrape the mixture into a container with a lid and store in the freezer until ready to use.

To serve, place a scoop of vanilla ice cream in each of 6 serving bowls. Scrape the granita to loosen it and spoon approximately ¹/₂ cup over each portion of vanilla ice cream.

SERVES 6

¹/₂ cup sugar
Freshly squeezed and strained juice from 12 blood oranges (about 3 cups)
Finely grated zest of 1 blood orange

WINTER

I need more than comfort food tonight

BRAISED SHORT RIBS WITH CHOCOLATE AND CINNAMON
CREAMY GRITS WITH PUREED CELERY ROOT
STEAMED BROCCOLI RABE
PROFITEROLES WITH BANANA RUM ICE CREAM AND BITTER CHOCOLATE SAUCE

I once told my therapist that sometimes when I am upset, eating a piece of chocolate can make me feel better. She explained that chocolate, if consumed in small amounts, has an ingredient that acts as a sedative. I realize that this doesn't mean I should eat chocolate every time my emotional weather changes, but it did make me think that when I require comfort food, chocolate has to figure in it somehow.

Chocolate has a long, culinary history in savory dishes. In France, schoolchildren still have a piece of chocolate tucked inside their baguettes. There is even a French wine called "Maury" made specifically to drink with chocolate. In Mexico, it is used in savory sauces. And in Italy I was once served pieces of bittersweet chocolate with Parmigiano.

This menu combines many of the foods I find most comforting. Of course, chocolate plays a starring role.

9 hours advance preparation

SERVES 6

3 pounds beef short ribs, on the bone, cut into 4-inch lengths

Sea salt and freshly ground black pepper, for seasoning

4 ounces slab bacon, sliced into ¼-inch lardons

1 onion, peeled and finely diced

2 whole cloves garlic, peeled

1 tablespoon all-purpose flour

1 cup dry sherry

1 quart beef stock or broth, plus more for serving

1 bouquet garni made with 2 bay leaves, 2 thyme sprigs, and 2 parsley sprigs

2 ounces bittersweet chocolate, grated or coarsely chopped

1 cinnamon stick, 4 inches long

This recipe was inspired by one in Coleman Andrews' book CATALAN CUISINE. I have had chocolate in meat dishes but never in beef stew. Coleman's recipe called for beef stew meat. I like it with short ribs, and it is terrific with grits (recipe follows) on a snowy winter day.

Trim any excess fat off the short ribs, and season them generously with salt and pepper. Cover and refrigerate for 4 hours. Remove from the refrigerator and, using kitchen string, tie each short rib in a bundle (this will keep the meat from falling off the bone while cooking).

In a large casserole or Dutch oven, cook the bacon, stirring constantly, over low heat until golden brown, about 5 minutes. Using a slotted spoon, transfer the bacon to paper towels to absorb the excess fat. Raise the heat to medium, add the short ribs, bone side up, and brown in the bacon fat. Remove the short ribs and set aside. Add the onion and garlic and cook for 1 minute. Whisk in the flour, then the sherry. Add the short ribs, bone side up, and then the bacon, 1 quart stock, and bouquet garni. Season with salt and pepper.

Cover and simmer the short ribs for 2 hours, stirring occasionally. After 1½ hours of cooking, add the chocolate and the cinnamon stick, and continue cooking for the final ½ hour, covered. Remove from the heat.

Let the short ribs cool in the pot and then refrigerate for 2 hours or overnight. (I always think they taste better the next day and it is easier to remove the excess fat.) Remove from the refrigerator, scrape off the fat in the casserole, and remove the kitchen string.

To serve, reheat the short ribs over low heat. Add a little extra beef stock if you want to thin out the sauce.

CREAMY GRITS WITH PUREED CELERY ROOT

Requires 2 hour advance preparation if not using instant grits

Grits go well with so many kinds of food that it's astonishing to find that they still don't get the attention they deserve. There is a wide variety of grits, each with a subtly different taste and texture. Years ago, I'm told, it was not unusual in the south to cook different kinds of grits for each day of the week.

Instead of using the highly processed supermarket variety, try a specialty version like the one from Anson Mills in Charleston, South Carolina (see Sources). It requires longer, slower cooking, but will reward you with a robust corn flavor, a creamy finish, and even a hint of lilac and violet that go perfectly with short ribs here.

Pour the water, milk, and 1 teaspoon salt into a large saucepan and bring it almost to a boil. Stir in the grits, reduce the heat, cover, and simmer for about 1½ hours, stirring frequently. If the grits become too dry before they are cooked through, just add a little water from time to time. They are done when they are chewy, not hard, when you bite into them. (If using instant grits, follow the cooking directions on the package.)

Put the celery root, 1 teaspoon salt, and the lemon juice in a medium saucepan. Add water to cover the celery root by 2 inches, cover the pot, and bring to a boil. Cook until the celery root is tender when pierced with a small knife, 12 to 15 minutes. Drain and let cool. Then puree it through a food mill (you should have 2 cups of puree).

Stir the celery root puree, butter, and heavy cream into the grits. Cook, covered, over very low heat for 15 minutes, stirring frequently. (If using instant grits, stir in the celery root puree, butter, and heavy cream, and cook uncovered for 2 to 3 minutes or until heated through.) Season with salt and pepper to taste, and serve.

SERVES 6 TO 8

2 cups water

1 cup milk

2 teaspoons sea salt, plus more for seasoning

1 cup Anson grits

2 small celery root bulbs (about 2 pounds), each one peeled and cut into eighths

Freshly squeezed juice from 1 lemon

2 tablespoons unsalted butter

¼ cup heavy cream

Freshly ground white pepper

STEAMED BROCCOLI RABE

The bitterness of broccoli rabe is perfect with the short-ribs and grits.

Trim 2 inches off the stems of the broccoli rabe. Cut the remaining broccoli rabe into 3-inch pieces. Place it in a colander and rinse. Bring the water in a steamer to a boil and then add the broccoli rabe. Sprinkle with the salt, cover, and steam for 4 minutes. Remove the cover and, using kitchen tongs, transfer the broccoli to a serving bowl. Drizzle with the olive oil and serve.

SERVES 8

2 bunches broccoli rabe

1 teaspoon sea salt

1 tablespoon extra-virgin olive oil

AS ALWAYS A WONDER-
FUL DINNER (BREAKFAST
+ LUNCH!) I HAD THE
BEST NIGHT. NEXT TIME
AT MY PLACE. I'LL TRY.
MANY MANY THANKS XJ.

PROFITEROLES WITH BANANA RUM ICE CREAM AND BITTER CHOCOLATE SAUCE

SERVES 6

BANANA RUM ICE CREAM

3 cups heavy cream

1 cup whole milk

¾ cup sugar

1 vanilla bean, split in half lengthwise

7 egg yolks

4 very ripe bananas, pureed (2 cups)

¼ cup dark rum

PÂTE À CHOUX

⅓ cup water

4 tablespoons unsalted butter, cut into small pieces

2 tablespoons milk

1 teaspoon sugar

⅛ teaspoon salt

½ cup all-purpose flour

2 eggs

BITTER CHOCOLATE SAUCE

6 ounces bittersweet chocolate, chopped into small pieces

¾ cup heavy cream, plus more for thinning

2 tablespoons unsalted butter

½ teaspoon vanilla extract

Requires 4 hours advance preparation if making your own ice cream

The first time I ordered profiteroles was in a restaurant in Paris. I thought I was just ordering a simple dessert, but what showed up was quite an impressive presentation—and delicious, to boot. The waiter came out with two perfect pâte à choux, each filled with several small scoops of ice cream. He then poured a warm chocolate sauce over the profiteroles—at what seemed at the time about three feet away from my dish. He then brought slightly whipped cream, which he left on the table. That memory has never left me and I have never treated a profiterole as just another simple dessert since.

Profiteroles can change like chameleons—the flavor of the ice cream can reflect the season—and are great for dinner parties because most of the preparation can be done in advance. The combination of bananas and chocolate makes the perfect comfort food, too.

If you really want to go for it, top with whipped cream. This recipe can be easily doubled. Be sure to serve the chocolate sauce warm.

MAKE THE BANANA RUM ICE CREAM: Combine the cream, milk, sugar, and vanilla bean in a medium saucepan. Cook over medium-high heat, stirring, until the sugar is dissolved and the milk is warm, 125 degrees.

Fill a large bowl with ice water and place a metal bowl large enough to hold the cream mixture in it. Whisk the egg yolks for 1 minute in a large bowl. Remove the vanilla from the cream and scrape the seeds back into the cream. Slowly pour a little warm cream into the eggs, whisking as you pour. Continue stirring in the rest of the cream. Once you have added all the cream, pour the mixture into the saucepan. Bring the mixture to a medium-high simmer, stirring continuously, until the mixture thickens, coats the back of a spoon, and is 170 degrees. Remove the mixture from the heat and immediately pour it through a sieve into the metal bowl in the ice bath. Stir the mixture for several minutes to speed the cooling.

Using an electric mixer, beat the banana puree and the rum until smooth. Whisk the banana mixture into the cream mixture. Stir until cool. Refrigerate for at least 3 hours, then freeze in an ice-cream maker according to the manufacturer's instructions.

MAKE THE PÂTE À CHOUX: Preheat the oven to 400 degrees. In a 2-quart, heavy-duty saucepan combine the water, butter, milk, sugar, and salt, and bring to a high simmer until the milk mixture is scalding, stirring until the butter is completely melted. Remove the pan from the heat. Add all the flour at once and, using a wooden spoon, stir until the mixture is a thick paste. Return the saucepan to low heat and cook, stirring, for 1 minute to dry out the mixture.

Transfer the choux paste to the bowl of an electric mixer. Using the paddle attachment, beat the mixture at low speed for 1 minute to cool it down. Add the eggs, one at a time, mixing after each addition. The dough should be soft and sticky.

Fit a pastry bag with a plain $1/4$-inch round tip. Fill the bag with the choux paste. Line a baking sheet with parchment paper. Pipe out the choux paste 1 inch apart into rounds 2 inches in diameter and about $1/2$-inch high. You should have 18 in total.

Bake the pâte à choux in the preheated oven for 15 minutes, then reduce the heat to 300 degrees and bake until golden brown, 10 to 15 minutes. Remove the profiteroles from the oven and place on a rack to cool. Turn them over and gently pierce the bottom of each profiterole with a sharp knife. Reserve.

MAKE THE CHOCOLATE SAUCE: Place the chocolate, cream, butter, and vanilla in the top of a double boiler or metal bowl set over simmering water. Melt gently, then stir until smooth. If you want a thinner sauce, add a bit more cream. Be careful not to overheat the sauce or it will seize up. If it does, just stir in more cream. Serve warm.

ASSEMBLE THE PROFITEROLES: Cut the profiteroles in half crosswise. Scoop some ice cream into each bottom half. Replace the tops and place 3 on each of the 6 dessert plates. Pour some warm chocolate sauce over them, and serve.

Did someone say fire?

ARUGULA WITH TOASTED HAZELNUTS AND PECORINO CHEESE
GRILLED ALSATIAN PIZZA
GRILLED BUTTERNUT SQUASH, FONTINA, AND ROSEMARY PIZZA
GRILLED PINEAPPLE UPSIDE-DOWN CAKE WITH RUM SAUCE

Not much can stop a passionate griller such as myself. Not bad weather. Not even life in a big city apartment—though that certainly presented a serious problem until I discovered the Tuscan grill (see Sources). Life hasn't been quite the same since I began using one in my living room fireplace. At first I was unstoppable, grilling every day even into the spring. Whether toasting bread, baking beans, or slow cooking a stew, I discovered that everything tasted better straight from the fire.

And then one fine warm day when I was stoking the fire to make grilled chicken for a friend from out of town, there was a knock on the door. A nervous neighbor appeared and asked, "Hey, Is there a fire in your apartment?" "Just making lunch," I replied. He left confused, but I knew that it was time to put away the grill until fall, when the colder weather merits a little chimney smoke.

Besides being a lot of fun, grilling in your living room or kitchen is easy and bound to impress your friends. I make so many different things on the grill that it was hard to pick just a few for this chapter.

Another item that is essential in my kitchen—and doesn't require opening the chimney flue—is my peppermill designed specifically for grinding whole dried chilis. Dried red chili flakes are banned from my larder because they loose their flavor and become stale very quickly. There is nothing better than freshly ground chili pepper (see Sources), which adds the perfect note of heat to my pizzas.

ARUGULA WITH TOASTED HAZELNUTS AND PECORINO CHEESE

SERVES 4

2 teaspoons sherry vinegar

3 tablespoons extra-virgin olive oil

1 teaspoon sea salt

Freshly ground black peppercorns to taste

¼ pound arugula leaves, washed and dried

½ cup hazelnuts, toasted and coarsely chopped

2 ounces Pecorino cheese, thinly shaved

The combination of the peppery arugula, the toasted nuttiness of the hazelnuts, and the salty Pecorino cheese make this a hearty salad for cold winter nights.

In a small bowl, whisk together the sherry vinegar, olive oil, salt, and pepper. Drizzle in the oil, whisking constantly.

In a salad bowl toss the arugula with the vinaigrette. Divide the salad among 4 serving plates. Scatter the hazelnuts evenly over the arugula. Top with the shaved Pecorino, and serve.

GRILLED ALSATIAN PIZZA

MAKES 2 12-BY-9-INCH PIZZAS

1 recipe Pizza Dough

1 cup fromage blanc

²/3 cup grated Gruyère cheese

1 egg

1 tablespoon all-purpose flour

¼ pound slab bacon, sliced into ¼-inch lardons

2 medium onions, peeled and thinly sliced (about 5 cups)

Olive oil

Sea salt and freshly ground black pepper

Freshly ground dried chilis, to taste

¼ cup fresh parsley leaves, coarsley chopped

Requires 3 hours advance preparation

This is an interpretation of the classic Alsatian tart flambé. If you cannot find fromage blanc, it is very easy to make (see following recipe), but requires a 12-hour lead-time.

Prepare the Pizza Dough (see following recipe).

Put the fromage blanc, grated Gruyère cheese, egg, and flour in a bowl and mix until well blended. Cover and refrigerate until ready to use.

In a large skillet, cook the bacon lardons over medium-high heat until golden brown. Using a slotted spoon, remove the bacon from the skillet and reserve. Add the onions and cook in the bacon fat over low heat until soft, about 5 minutes. Remove the onions and reserve.

Heat your grill and grill rack, and preheat the oven to 450 degrees. Place one 12-by-9-inch pizza dough oval on a floured pizza paddle or on a floured inverted baking sheet. When your grill is hot, gently slide the dough onto the grill, and gently brush the top with olive oil. Within a minute the dough will begin to puff. Grill for 1 to 2 minutes more. With tongs, lift the edge of the dough to check the color underneath. When the dough becomes golden brown and you see grill marks, flip the dough over. Brush the grilled side with olive oil and grill the second side for 1 to 2 minutes until the dough is golden brown on both sides. Repeat with the other pizza dough oval.

To assemble and finish the pizza, place the grilled dough on a baking sheet. Spread it with half the fromage blanc mixture, leaving a ³/4-inch border around the edge of the pizza. Top with half of the onion slices, and half the bacon lardons.

Place 1 pizza in the preheated oven for 5–8 minutes or until the cheese has melted. Remove from the oven and top with salt, black pepper and freshly ground dried chilis, and half of the chopped parsley. Slice and serve immediately. Repeat with the other pizza.

FROMAGE BLANC

Put the ricotta, yogurt, and salt in a blender and puree for 30 seconds. Pour into a bowl, cover, and refrigerate for 12 hours. It keeps for up to 2 weeks refrigerated.

3/4 cups fresh whole milk ricotta cheese
2 tablespoons plain whole milk yogurt
Pinch of sea salt

PIZZA DOUGH

Requires 3 hours advance preparation
This recipe makes enough dough for two 12-by-9-inch pizzas.

When I grill pizza over wood or charcoal, I start my fire at least 1 hour before my dough has risen the second time. Your fire needs plenty of hot embers to grill the pizza dough evenly. If you are baking the pizza, preheat your oven at least 20 minutes before you are ready to bake the pizza.

1 1/2 cups warm water
1/4-ounce envelope active dry yeast
1 pinch sugar
3 1/2 cups all-purpose flour
2 teaspoons salt
1 tablespoon plus 2 teaspoons extra-virgin olive oil

Combine the warm water, yeast, and sugar in a small bowl and stir until the yeast dissolves, 3 to 5 minutes. Combine 3 cups of the flour and the salt on a work surface. Make a well, then add the yeast mixture and 1 tablespoon of the oil. Knead the dough until firm and elastic, 10 to 15 minutes, adding additional flour if needed.

Grease a large bowl with 1 teaspoon of the oil. Shape the dough into a ball, add to the bowl, and turn to coat it completely with the oil. Cover the bowl with plastic wrap and place it in a warm spot until the dough has doubled in size, 2 to 2 1/2 hours.

Punch the dough down, divide it in half, and shape it into 2 balls. Oil another large bowl with the remaining 1 teaspoon oil. Place one dough ball in each bowl and rotate them to coat them completely with the oil. Cover both bowls with plastic wrap and let the dough rise in a warm draft-free spot for 1 hour or until doubled in size.

When doubled in size, punch the dough down again. Flatten out each ball on a lightly floured surface. Using your hands, gently press and stretch out each piece of dough into an oval approximately 1/2-inch thick and 12 by 9 inches in diameter. Be careful not to overwork the dough.

GRILLED BUTTERNUT SQUASH, FONTINA, AND ROSEMARY PIZZA

Requires 3 hours advance preparation

Prepare the Pizza Dough (see page 155).

Preheat the oven to 350 degrees. Cut the butternut squash in half lengthwise and brush the cut sides with olive oil. Place the squash cut side down on a parchment-lined baking sheet and bake for 1 hour and 30 minutes. Remove from the oven. When cool enough to handle, peel the skin off the squash. Slice lengthwise into $\frac{1}{2}$-inch slices. Reserve.

Increase the oven temperature to 425 degrees. Heat your grill and grill rack. Place one 12-by-9-inch pizza dough round on a floured pizza paddle or on a floured inverted baking sheet.

When your grill is hot, gently slide the dough onto the grill and brush the top with olive oil. Within a minute the dough will begin to puff. Grill for 1 to 2 minutes more. With tongs, lift the edge of the dough to check the color underneath. When the underside of the dough becomes golden brown and you see grill marks, flip the dough over. Grill for 1 minute longer and remove the grilled dough with the pizza paddle. Repeat with the other pizza dough round.

Brush the first grilled side with olive oil and spread half the fontina evenly on top. Then lay half of the squash slices over the cheese and sprinkle with half of the rosemary and Parmigiano. Drizzle with olive oil and slide the pizza back onto the grill. Grill for 2 minutes longer. Season with salt and freshly ground dried chiles to taste. Slice and serve immediately. Repeat with the other pizza.

MAKES TWO, 12-BY-9-INCH PIZZAS

1 recipe Pizza Dough

1 small butternut squash
(about 2 pounds)

Olive oil, for brushing

$\frac{1}{2}$ pound fontina cheese, grated

2 tablespoons rosemary leaves,
coarsely chopped

$\frac{1}{4}$ cup grated Parmigiano cheese

Salt and freshly ground dried chiles

This classic America dessert is delicious with its rum-soaked pineapple. If you cannot grill the pineapple, it is still wonderful. The remaining pineapple is great, sliced thin, soaked in rum, and sprinkled with chopped fresh tarragon.

SERVES 8

CAKE

½ fresh pineapple, cut lengthwise
1 cup dark rum
1 stick (4 ounces) unsalted butter
¾ cup packed dark brown sugar
¼ cup pecans, chopped
2 large eggs, at room temperature
½ cup milk
1 cup all-purpose flour
¾ cup granulated sugar
1½ teaspoons baking powder
¼ teaspoon salt

RUM SAUCE

1 stick (4 ounces) unsalted butter
1 cup packed light brown sugar
¼ cup rum reserved form the macerated pineapple (above)
2 tablespoons water
1 teaspoon vanilla extract
1 large egg

MAKE THE CAKE: Peel the pineapple and remove the center core slice off the center core. Slice in half lengthwise then crosswise into ½-inch slices. Place the pineapple pieces in a shallow nonreactive bowl and pour the rum on top. Let macerate for 1 hour at room temperature. Drain the pineapple, reserving ¼ cup plus 2 tablespoons of the rum.

Heat your grill. When hot, grill the pineapple slices until golden brown, about 4 to 5 minutes per side. Transfer to a bowl and reserve.

Preheat the oven to 350 degrees. In a 9-inch baking pan or skillet, melt 4 tablespoon of the butter over low heat. Coat all the sides of the pan. Sprinkle the brown sugar evenly over the bottom of the pan, then sprinkle the pecans evenly over the brown sugar. Arrange as many slices of pineapple in a single layer on top of the brown sugar as you are able to fit. Drizzle 2 tablespoons of the reserved rum over the pineapple.

In a small saucepan, melt the remaining 4 tablespoons butter. Transfer to a small bowl and whisk in the eggs and milk. Set aside. In a large bowl, mix together the flour, granulated sugar, baking powder, and salt. Using an electric mixer, gradually stir in the egg mixture. Beat for 2 minutes at low speed. Spread the batter evenly over the pineapple.

Bake the cake in the preheated oven until golden brown and a toothpick inserted in center comes out clean, 35 to 40 minutes. Remove the pan from the oven and let cool for 5 minutes on a wire rack. Run a knife around edge of pan to loosen; shake the pan on the counter from side to side, then cover with a large plate and invert. Serve warm with the rum sauce.

MAKE THE RUM SAUCE: Melt the butter in a small saucepan. Add the brown sugar, reserved rum, water, and vanilla, and cook over medium-low heat until the sugar is dissolved, about 2 minutes.

Remove the sauce from the heat. Beat the egg in a bowl until frothy. Quickly mix the egg into the sauce and place the sauce back on the heat, stirring, until it thickens, about 1 minute. Serve immediately with the upside-down cake.

You buy Prada, I buy truffles

SHAVED BLACK TRUFFLES ON TOAST

TRUFFLED PORK CRÉPINETTES

PAN-FRIED CHICKEN BREAST WITH POTATO PUREE AND BLACK TRUFFLE GRAVY

POTATOES COOKED IN EMBERS

SHAVED BLACK TRUFFLES OVER TELEME CHEESE

CRÈME BRÛLÉE INFUSED WITH BLACK TRUFFLES

Luxury is in the eye of the beholder. To some of my friends it is a pair of Prada shoes or an Hèrmes handbag. Luxury for me is getting an exceptional ingredient at the peak of its season.

For most food people, the ultimate in luxurious ingredients is a white truffle from Alba or a black one from the Perigord region in France. I have often flown back from Italy with a truffle in my backpack while my friends, carrying their Prada purchases, express dismay at how much money I have spent. My response? "Hon, this truffle is a lot harder to find and is still a lot less expensive than your shoes."

When truffles are at their best they are poetic and surpass any taste in my experience. When they are not at their best, they are suddenly too expensive. They are subject to the whims of nature; there are good seasons for them and bad ones. The shame is that they are often sold when they are not at their peak and that gives them a bad name.

White truffles are meant to be eaten raw and should be shaved on a dish after they have been cooked. Unlike their Italian cousins, black truffles can be cooked, and there is nothing like the way they infuse a dish. But they too can be eaten raw. I once had a salad with a black truffle in the vinaigrette and could not believe how well the truffle flavor came through. My most memorable truffle, just for sheer decadence, was served at the restaurant Boyer in Reims, France. They baked a whole black truffle in pastry and served it with a rich truffle sauce. Recently my friend William Rubel showed me his favorite way of preparing black truffles. Just throw them on the embers in your fire, dust them off and eat them. Pretty risky, but if you have several on hand you might give his method a try.

I worried about basing a menu on such an expensive ingredient but eventually decided that truffles are so important to me they had to be included. I have chosen black truffles, saving the white ones for my next book. So one day when you find yourself in the company of a black truffle, here are some ideas of what to do with it (see Sources).

SHAVED BLACK TRUFFLES ON TOAST

SERVES 6 TO 8

1 black truffle (about 1 ounce)

¼ cup extra-virgin olive oil

1 baguette, sliced into 20 ¼-inch slices

Fleur de sel (see page 28)

One February, my dear friend Bruno Borie arrived from Bordeaux bearing a box with four huge black truffles. When he opened it in my kitchen, I almost fainted from excitement. First the smell, then the size, then the fact they were in my kitchen! Our meal that night consisted of a series of truffle courses and I think the most memorable of them was this appetizer.

There are a few tools for shaving truffles that I highly recommend. The first is a truffle shaver—a paddle with an adjustable serrated blade. A Japanese mandoline also works well for this task (see Sources). If you have a frozen truffle, use a microplane grater and always shave or grate the truffle while still frozen.

With a truffle shaver or mandoline, slice the truffle very thinly into a bowl. Add the extra-virgin olive oil. Make sure that all the truffle slices are covered in oil. Let this mixture sit for 1 hour.

Preheat the broiler. Place the baguette slices on a baking sheet and brush them with the truffle soaking oil. Place 2 truffle slices on each baguette, put the tray in the preheated oven, and broil for 1 minute or until the edges of the baguette are golden. Sprinkle with fleur de sel and serve immediately. Save any extra oil!!!

TRUFFLED PORK CRÉPINETTES

SERVES 6

¼ pound caul fat

1 tablespoon white wine vinegar

1 ¼ pounds pork shoulder or pork butt ground with ¼ pound fatback

1 clove garlic, peeled and minced

1 shallot, finely diced

2 tablespoons fresh thyme leaves

2 tablespoons chopped fresh sage leaves

1 ounce fresh black truffles, shaved into thin slices

1 teaspoon sea salt

2 teaspoons quatre-épices

1 tablespoon olive oil

Crépinettes are handmade sausages, shaped into small, flattened discs that can be made without having to use a casing. I like to season these with quatre-épices, a French blend of finely ground spices. Quatre-épices can be found in specialty food stores but you can easily make your own: Grind 1 tablespoon of white peppercorns, 1 teaspoon whole cloves, 1 teaspoon nutmeg, and 1 3-inch piece of cinnamon in an electric coffee or spice grinder. Often I just serve the crépinettes with fresh oysters or with a simple green salad, or both.

Cover the caul fat with tepid water and the white vinegar. Set aside. Combine all the other ingredients in a large bowl. Drain the caul fat and cut it into 5-inch squares with a pair of kitchen scissors.

Divide the pork mixture into 12 equal pieces and shape each one into an oval. Place each patty in the center of a piece of caul fat and wrap it up, tucking any excess fat underneath.

Heat a skillet, over medium-low heat and add the olive oil. Fry the crépinettes for 6 minutes each side. Serve immediately.

PAN-FRIED CHICKEN BREAST WITH POTATO PURÉE AND BLACK TRUFFLE GRAVY

SERVES 6

2 black truffles, cleaned (about 2 ounces)
6 chicken breasts, boned with skin (6 to 7 ounces each)
2 tablespoons all-purpose flour
1 teaspoon sea salt
1/4 teaspoon freshly ground black pepper
3 1/2 tablespoons cold unsalted butter
1 tablespoon extra-virgin olive oil

Requires 4 hours advance preparation if making the chicken stock

With a truffle shaver or mandoline, slice the truffle into thin slices. Cut 1 1/2 tablespoons butter into 1/8-inch cubes. Gently lift the skin off each chicken breast and slide several truffle slices and 1/4 tablespoon each of the diced butter under the skin. Cover the chicken and refrigerate for 2 hours or up to 24 hours before using.

Preheat the oven to 350 degrees. Remove the chicken breasts from the refrigerator. On a large plate, combine the flour, salt, and pepper. Dust both sides of the chicken breasts with the flour, shaking off any excess. Melt the remaining 2 tablespoons butter with the olive oil in a skillet large enough to hold all the chicken breasts. (Or cook the chicken in two batches.) When the oil in the pan starts to bubble, add the chicken breasts skin side down and cook over medium-high heat until the skin is golden brown, 2 to 3 minutes. Turn and cook the chicken on the other side for 2 minutes.

Place the chicken breasts on a parchment-lined baking sheet and bake in the preheated oven until very firm to the touch, 20–30 minutes. Remove from the oven and serve the chicken with the potato purée and the black truffle gravy (See below).

POTATO PUREE

SERVES 6

4 pounds medium Yukon gold potatoes
1 teaspoon sea salt, plus more for seasoning
3 tablespoons unsalted butter, cut into 1/2-inch cubes
1/4 cup chicken stock (see page 163)
1 cup heavy cream
Freshly ground white pepper

When I make mashed potatoes, I prefer to steam, rather than boil, them. If you don't have a steamer, improvise by placing a colander in a large pot and covering it tightly with aluminum foil once the water boils. I also put the potatoes through a food mill (see Sources) instead of mashing them. This makes them much lighter.

Peel the potatoes and cut them into 1 1/2-inch cubes. Put them in a steamer in an even layer and sprinkle with the salt. Bring the water to a boil. Once the water has boiled, cover the steamer and cook for about 25 minutes or until the potatoes are tender when pierced with a sharp knife. When the potatoes are cool enough to handle, put them in a food mill and puree.

Put the butter, stock, and cream in a large saucepan and bring to a high simmer. Gently stir in the potato puree. Continue stirring until the potatoes are heated through. Season with salt and pepper to taste. Serve immediately.

BLACK TRUFFLE GRAVY

You can make this recipe with regular chicken stock, but the reduced stock gives the gravy a deeper and richer flavor. If you have time you can grate ½ ounce of the truffle, add it to the heavy cream, and let the mixture sit in the refrigerator overnight. The truffle will infuse the cream and your gravy will have a more intense truffle flavor.

Melt the butter in a saucepan over medium heat. Add the flour and cook, whisking until golden brown, 1 to 2 minutes. Slowly whisk in the reduced chicken stock, and cook, whisking constantly until the gravy thickens, 10 to 12 minutes. Stir in the heavy cream and grated truffle. Season with salt and pepper. Serve immediately.

MAKES 3 CUPS

2 tablespoons unsalted butter

2 tablespoons all-purpose flour

2½ cups Reduced Chicken Stock or regular chicken stock (see below)

½ cup heavy cream

1 black truffle (about 1 ounce), cleaned and coarsely grated

Sea salt and freshly ground black pepper to taste

CHICKEN STOCK

Requires 4 hours advance preparation.
The Black Truffle Gravy calls for reduced chicken stock. Reducing a stock simply means simmering it over a medium-low heat, until half of it has evaporated, see below.

Put the chicken, onion, garlic, carrots, celery, bouquet garni, cloves, and salt in a large stockpot. Add the water. Bring to a boil, reduce the heat, and simmer for 2 hours, skimming from time to time. Take the stock off the heat and let it cool for 10 minutes. Pour the stock through a sieve into a large container. (You should have 6 quarts.)

MAKE REDUCED CHICKEN STOCK: Pour the strained stock into a stockpot and bring it to a boil. Reduce the heat and simmer, skimming occasionally, until the stock is reduced by half, about 2 hours. Remove the reduced stock from the heat, let cool, and reserve. (The stock can be refrigerated for up to 3 days or frozen for up to one month.)

MAKES 6 QUARTS

1 whole chicken (about 3½ to 4 pounds)

1 medium onion, peeled and studded with 3 cloves garlic, peeled

2 carrots, peeled and cut into 1-inch lengths (about 2 cups)

2 stalks celery, cut into 2-inch lengths (about 2 cups)

1 bouquet garni made with 4 sprigs parsley, 4 sprigs thyme, and 1 bay leaf, tied in cheesecloth

4 whole cloves

1 teaspoon coarse sea salt

8 quarts cold water

POTATOES COOKED IN EMBERS

Requires 1 hour advance preparation

There is nothing simpler than baking a potato in the embers of your fireplace. The potatoes take on a subtle smoky flavor. Since truffles and potatoes are a sublime pairing, I wanted to offer another option besides the potato puree to serve with the truffle gravy.

Make a bed of embers on one side of your fireplace. Place the raw potatoes directly on the bed of embers, then cover the potatoes with additional embers. Continue the fire in the fireplace to one side or just off center. This will enable you to continually add more embers if necessary throughout the cooking process.

The potatoes are done when they are easily pierced with a knife, about 30 minutes. Remove the potatoes from the embers. Brush the embers off the potatoes and place them on individual serving dishes. Slice in half, sprinkle with fleur de sel, and drizzle with the gravy. You can also scoop the potato out from its skin and serve it on individual plates sprinkled with the salt and drizzled with the gravy.

SERVES 4

4 baking potatoes, about ½ pound each
1 teaspoon fleur de sel (see page 28)
Black Truffle Gravy (recipe page 163)

SHAVED BLACK TRUFFLES OVER TELEME CHEESE

Requires 24 hours advance preparation

This is a wonderful recipe for the holiday season as it lasts for at least a week and you can bring it out each time you have guests. I like to order a whole Teleme, which weighs about 5 pounds (see Sources). When it is perfectly ripe, I peel off some of the top layer and place several small black truffles over it. I then cover the whole thing with plastic wrap and leave it in a cool place for 24 hours to infuse. To serve, I spoon some of the truffled cheese onto individual plates and add a few more truffle shavings. You can, however, also just buy the amount of cheese you need for one meal using the same process. Serve it with thinly sliced toasted walnut bread.

Spoon 1 large tablespoon of fresh ripe Teleme cheese (about one ounce) onto 4 individual plates. Shave several slices of black truffle directly over each portion of cheese. Serve with the bread.

SERVES 4

4 ounces ripe Teleme cheese
1 freshly shaved black truffle
4 slices walnut bread, toasted

CRÈME BRÛLÉE INFUSED WITH BLACK TRUFFLES

Requires 5 hours advance preparation

MAKES 6 INDIVIDUAL DESSERTS

3 cups heavy cream
1 cup plus 6 tablespoons sugar
*1 small black truffle (about ½ ounce),
finely grated*
3 whole eggs plus 4 egg yolks

The infusion of black truffles in this crème brûlée creates a subtle elegant flavor. A microplane grater (see Sources), which provides a fine grating, is important for this recipe.

Crème brûlées are best made in wide shallow ramekin molds.

I have never had success caramelizing crème brûlées under a broiler. Broiling tends to cook the custard before caramelizing. I use a small butane torch available in most specialty kitchen shops (see Sources).

Preheat the oven to 250 degrees. Place the 6 ½-cup ramekins in a baking pan with sides at least 2 inches high.

In a 4-quart saucepan cook the heavy cream, 1 cup of the sugar, and the grated black truffle over very low heat, stirring, until the sugar has dissolved. Remove from the heat and let cool, then refrigerate for at least 2 hours or overnight so the truffle flavor will infuse the cream.

In a medium saucepan bring the truffle mixture to a simmer over low heat. Whisk together the eggs and egg yolks in a large bowl. Slowly whisk in 2 cups of the truffle mixture, whisking constantly so the eggs won't curdle. Gently add this mixture to the truffle mixture remaining in the saucepan and cook slowly until the custard coats your spoon, 8 to 12 minutes. Remove from the heat and strain the mixture through a fine sieve.

Fill a kettle with water and bring to a boil. Keep the water hot until ready to bake the brûlées. Divide the custard evenly among the 6 ramekins. Place the baking pan in the oven. Carefully pour boiling water into the pan so the water comes about halfway up the sides of the ramekins and cook the custards for 35 to 40 minutes. The custards are ready when you tap on the side of the ramekin and the texture is firm and does not jiggle. Remove the pan from the oven very carefully so as not to spill the water. Slide a spatula under each ramekin and carefully place the custards on a rack to cool, then refrigerate them for at least 3 hours and up to 24 hours before glazing.

Remove the custards from the refrigerator and place them on a work surface. Sprinkle the remaining 6 tablespoons sugar evenly on top. Hold a small butane torch, approximately 8 inches above the custards and pass evenly back and forth across the tops, until the sugar caramelizes and becomes dark brown.

Serve immediately (or refrigerate for up to 2 hours before serving).

A diet that works for me

POACHED COD WITH FENNEL, CARROTS, AND POTATOES
BOSC PEARS WITH FLEUR DE SEL
FRESH ROSEMARY INFUSION

Let's face it, we live in a culture of the diet obsessed. Everything we read tells us what to eat, what not to, and what to combine with what to lose weight. Why do we have to take our frustrations out on food? Why do we have to consider bread the enemy and dieting a form of combat? Our minds may be the problem, but not food. I've been on a diet most of my life, and I've finally found one that works: Eat less but eat real. Sounds easy, and it works for me. That doesn't mean that I'll ever be skinny, but it means that I feel in control of how I eat and that I feel good about myself. That's what's important.

There are times that I feel the need to eat simply. But if I think of a meal as a diet I'll feel deprived before I start, so I make a dinner like this one that gives me a hit of healthy eating without the sense of deprivation.

POACHED COD WITH FENNEL, CARROTS, AND POTATOES

Requires 1 hour advance preparation

If you are not on a diet, serve the cod with garlic aioli (page 101). For a sublime flavor pairing with cod, add one quarter teaspoon of saffron to the aioli.

Don't get scared off by having to make fish stock. The homemade variety is worth the trouble and brings the soup to life. When making a fish stock, always rinse the bones well; remove gills and any extra skin since they will discolor the stock. I use bones from white fish, and if I have any shrimp, crab, or lobster shells I add them for extra flavor. Most fishmongers will sell or give you fish bones if you ask them in advance. If the fish stock is not to be used within 24 hours, cool it and freeze for up to three weeks.

Once a friend from the south told me you should never cut fish on wood or cook with wooden utensils because it spoils the fish, and I haven't since. Maybe it's because the fish will pick up flavors from the wood, I don't know for sure.

MAKE THE FISH STOCK: In a large stockpot, combine all the ingredients. Bring to a boil over high heat. Reduce the heat and simmer for 45 minutes, partially covered. Skim any impurities that rise to the top several times during cooking. Strain the stock through a fine-mesh sieve. (You should have approximately 3 quarts.)

PREPARE THE COD AND VEGETABLES: Put the fish stock in a large stockpot and bring it to a boil. Add the fennel wedges, carrots, and potatoes, reduce the heat, and simmer for 15 minutes. Remove the vegetables from the stock with a slotted spoon and place in a bowl.

Bring the stock back to a high simmer and add the cod pieces. Poach for 8 to 10 minutes until the cod is flaky and opaque. Return the vegetables to the pot and cook for 2 minutes. Remove the pot from the heat.

To serve, place 6 large soup bowls on the counter near the stove. Place a variety of vegetables in each bowl. Then place a piece of cod in the center of each bowl along with the vegetables. Ladle some of the hot broth over the fish and vegetables. Sprinkle with sea salt and freshly ground pepper. Chop 1 tablespoon of fennel fronds and garnish each bowl with some chopped fennel fronds. Serve immediately.

SERVES 6

FISH STOCK

3 quarts cold water

2 cups dry wine

4 pounds fish bones (from white fish only), heads, fins, and gills removed, and bones rinsed well

2 cups shrimp, crab, or lobster shells (optional)

1 large onion (about 1 pound), peeled and quartered

2 stalks celery, cut into 1-inch lengths (about 1 cup)

1 large carrot, peeled and cut into 1-inch lengths (about 1 cup)

1 whole head of garlic, cut crosswise

Fennel stalks cut from 1 fennel bulb (see fennel below), cut into 1-inch lengths (about 8 ounces)

1 stalk lemongrass (about 1 ounce), cut into 1/2-inch rounds

1 teaspoon fennel seeds

Bouquet garni, made with 1 bay leaf, 3 sprigs parsley and 3 sprigs fresh thyme tied in cheesecloth

1/4 teaspoon whole black peppercorns

COD AND VEGETABLES

1 bulb fresh fennel, cut lengthwise into sixths, fronds reserved for garnish and tops reserved for the stock

2 carrots, peeled and cut into 1-inch lengths

6 small potatoes, peeled and halved

6 6-ounce cod fillets

Sea salt and freshly ground black pepper to taste

BOSC PEARS WITH FLEUR DE SEL

SERVES 6

6 perfectly ripe Bosc pears

1 lemon, halved

1 tablespoon extra-virgin olive oil

1 1/2 teaspoons fleur de sel or any other fine sea salt

Bosc pears are rock hard until they are ripe. Then when they ripen, they go bad quickly so watch them carefully.

Peel the pears, slice in half vertically, and remove the cores. Place them cut side down on a chopping board and slice each pear half lengthwise into 10 slices. Fan 2 sliced pear halved on each of six serving plates. Sprinkle each portion with a squeeze of lemon juice, the olive oil, and 1/4 teaspoon fleur de sel. Serve.

FRESH ROSEMARY INFUSION

MAKES 6 CUPS

24-inch sprigs fresh rosemary, including stems

6 to 8 cups boiling water

Drinking a cup of hot water, infused or plain, helps you digest your food and feel full. In addition, rosemary aids the digestion of fat while you sleep. I always try to end a meal with this rosemary infusion.

Put the rosemary in a 6 to 8 cup glass infusion teapot or regular teapot. Add the boiling water and steep for 5 minutes. Serve immediately.

A hearty dish in the heart of winter

THOMAS KELLER'S VEGETABLE SPOON BREAD IN BRIOCHE CRUST
WATERCRESS AND AVOCADO SALAD WITH TOASTED SESAME VINAIGRETTE
PEAR CONFIT WITH COMTÉ CHEESE

Winter is often about concentrating your efforts on keeping warm, keeping going, and keeping entertained indoors. I like to focus on cooking for friends, and one of the best ways of doing this is to make a one-dish meal that puts together the best of the season's vegetables.

Thomas Keller's vegetable spoonbread is an example of a satisfying one-dish winter meal. Even though it takes a bit of time to make, it's preparation is straightforward and you can use whatever vegetables you have on hand. It also looks impressive, and like everything Keller does, it is delicious. If you are still hungry at the end of this meal, I have included a salad and a cheese course.

Requires 4 hours advance preparation

SERVES 6 TO 8

BRIOCHE DOUGH

3 sticks (³/₄ pound) cold unsalted butter,
cut into tablespoons

¹/₄-ounce envelopes active dry yeast

¹/₂ cup whole milk, warmed

4 whole eggs plus 2 egg yolks,
at room temperature

4 cups all-purpose flour, sifted

¹/₄ cup sugar

1 teaspoon sea salt

VEGETABLE FILLING

3 tablespoons olive oil

1 fennel bulb, core removed and thinly sliced

1 small Savoy cabbage, core removed and
thinly sliced

2 zucchini, cut into ¹/₄-inch rounds

3 carrots, peeled and finely diced

1 medium onion, peeled and thinly sliced

1 stalk celery, peeled and finely diced

1 leek, sliced into ¹/₄-inch rounds, soaked in
water and thoroughly rinsed

3 cloves garlic, peeled and minced

2 red bell peppers, seeded and finely diced

1 cup chicken or vegetable stock

¹/₂ cup dry white wine

1 bouquet garni made with 1 bay leaf,
4 sprigs parsley, and 2 sprigs thyme
tied in cheesecloth

Sea salt and freshly ground black pepper
to taste

2 tablespoons unsalted butter

2 cups assorted mushrooms, cleaned and
coarsely chopped

¹/₂ cup grated ricotta salata cheese

¹/₄ cup finely chopped mixed fresh herb
(such as sage, rosemary, oregano, thyme)

MAKE THE BRIOCHE DOUGH: Place the pieces of butter in between 2 sheets of plastic wrap and gently tap with a rolling pin to make pliable. Reserve at room temperature.

Stir the yeast into the warm milk until thoroughly dissolved. In a separate bowl, whisk together the eggs and yolks and then mix in the yeast mixture.

Using an electric mixer combine the flour, sugar, and salt. Add the egg mixture to the dry ingredients and combine thoroughly on low speed. Add the butter, 2 tablespoons at a time, and mix well after each addition until all the butter is incorporated. The dough should be fairly stiff with no crumbs present. If you have any crumbs, add a few drops of milk to absorb them. Do not overbeat.

Remove the dough from the bowl and place it on a lightly floured surface. Knead a few times by hand to make sure the butter is thoroughly incorporated. Put the dough in a large buttered bowl and cover with plastic wrap. Set aside in a warm spot for 3 hours or until doubled in bulk. Punch down the dough and refrigerate until ready to use.

MAKE THE VEGETABLE FILLING: Heat the olive oil in a large skillet. Add the fennel, cabbage, zucchini, carrots, onion, celery, leek, and garlic, and cook over medium-high heat until soft, about 5 minutes. Add the red peppers, stock, and wine, and bring to a simmer. Add the bouquet garni, salt, and pepper, and simmer the vegetables until soft and the liquid has almost evaporated, 15 to 20 minutes. Remove from the heat, and let cool.

In a large skillet, melt the butter over a medium heat. Add the mushrooms and a little salt and cook until nicely browned. Add the mushrooms to the other vegetables. Season with salt and pepper.

ASSEMBLE THE SPOONBREAD: Preheat the oven to 325 degrees. Remove the dough from the refrigerator and punch down. On a lightly floured surface, roll out the brioche dough into a 13-inch round. Use as little flour as possible. Refrigerate the round for ¹/₂ hour.

Coat a 9-inch skillet with vegetable oil or cooking spray. Remove the dough from the refrigerator and press it firmly into the bottom and sides of the skillet. Add the vegetable filling. The dough should peek over the top of the vegetables. Fold the edges of the dough over the vegetables.

Place the spoonbread in the preheated oven and bake until the dough is golden brown, 30 to 35 minutes. Sprinkle the ricotta salata evenly over the vegetables then the chopped herbs and serve.

WATERCRESS AND AVOCADO SALAD WITH TOASTED SESAME VINAIGRETTE

If you are still hungry, this salad provides a great contrast to the spoonbread. I find it a good course before cheese to clean the palate. The bitter watercress, the nuttiness of the toasted sesame seeds, and the creaminess of the avocado are a wonderful combination of flavors and textures.

Trim off and discard 3 inches from stems of the watercress. Wash and dry well. Refrigerate until ready to use.

Heat a small skillet over medium heat. Add the sesame seeds and toast for 1 minute or until they are light golden brown. Shake the skillet constantly so the seeds cook evenly and don't stick. Immediately scrape them into a small bowl. While the seeds are still warm, mix them with the sherry vinegar. Whisk in the olive oil gradually and season with the salt and pepper to taste.

To assemble the salad, place the watercress in a salad bowl. Add half the dressing and toss well. In a small bowl, gently toss the remaining dressing with the avocado. Add the dressed avocado to the salad and serve.

SERVES 6 TO 8

2 bunches watercress (about 1 pound)

2 tablespoons raw sesame seeds

1 tablespoon Spanish sherry vinegar

1/4 cup extra-virgin olive oil

1/2 teaspoon sea salt

Freshly ground black pepper

1 avocado, peeled, quartered, and sliced lengthwise into 1/2-inch slices

PEAR CONFIT WITH COMTÉ CHEESE

The flavor and texture of Comté cheese varies with its age. I prefer a young Comté with this Pear confit. Artisan Cheese in San Francisco is now importing Comté from Jean D'Alos, who is a wonderful Bordeaux affineur, someone who, besides selling cheeses also ages them in the shop's aging cellars. My rule of thumb is two ounces of cheese per person (see Sources).

When making the pear confit, I like to make extra. This recipe can easily be divided in half. The pear confit keeps for up to 1 week in the refrigerator.

Place all the ingredients except the cheese in an 8-quart stockpot. Bring to a boil, reduce the heat, and simmer on a diffuser, stirring occasionally, for 45 minutes to 1 hour or until the liquid has evaporated. Remove the sachet and let cool. Serve with the cheese.

SERVES 6

1 spice sachet made with 4 allspice berries, 4 whole cloves, and 1 3-inch cinnamon stick tied in cheesecloth

8 anjou pears, peeled, cored and cut into 1/4-inch dice

1 red bell pepper, halved, seeds discarded, and finely diced

1 red onion, peeled and minced

1/2 cup packed brown sugar

1/2 cup white wine vinegar

12 ounces Comté cheese

All dressed up, and staying home

CHAMPAGNE AND ELDERFLOWER COCKTAIL

CUCUMBER-INFUSED VODKA

MAKER'S MARK SOUR MADE WITH MEYER LEMON JUICE

LORA'S PUERTO RICAN EGGNOG

DRIED ORGANIC APRICOTS WITH MARCONA ALMONDS

ORANGE MARMALADE AND FRESH RICOTTA CHEESE ON AK MAK CRACKERS

DATES WITH AGED MANCHEGO CHEESE

ROSEMARY-AND-ORANGE-CURED OLIVES

OYSTER SHOOTERS WITH TABASCO AND GINGER VODKA

STEAMED SWEET RICE WITH CAVIAR

SMOKED SALMON ON NINE-GRAIN BREAD WITH DILL BUTTER

EDAMAME TOSSED WITH SEA SALT

CHOCOLATE AND ORANGE POT DE CRÉME

During the holidays I want nothing more than to give great dinner parties, but like everyone else, I am usually too busy to do it. So this is the time when I turn to cocktail parties. People can stop in or stay for the evening. I love a chic cocktail party and I think I have the formula for one.

My plan is to make sure the food includes interesting combinations and requires very little preparation. It's how you put the ingredients together that matters most. I always have three drinks that are so tempting it is hard for anyone to decide which one to try. And I make sure to offer something sweet as well. Over the years I have added to my cocktail repertoire but this menu includes my most successful standbys.

COCKTAILS

I don't believe in pouring wine at cocktail parties. I prefer my wine with a meal and I prefer sitting at a table to drink it. Of course if one of my guests wants a glass of wine it's always available. Here are a few of my favorite drinks for the holiday season, ending with a real treat, Puerto Rican eggnog. (I get requests as early as November for it.)

CHAMPAGNE AND ELDERFLOWER COCKTAIL

If you are serving a group of people, this cocktail is best made in batches, although you can also make one drink at a time. You do not need to spend a fortune on expensive champagne, but don't go for the cheapest either. I would choose a good-quality non-vintage Brut champagne and avoid sparkling wine, which is likely to be too sweet for the elderflower syrup. (See Sources for the elderflower syrup.)

MAKES 7 4-OUNCE COCKTAILS
¼ cup elderflower syrup
1 bottle (750 ml) champagne, chilled

Add the elderflower syrup to a pitcher. Slowly pour the whole bottle of champagne along the inside of the side of the pitcher to prevent the champagne from bubbling over. Stir, and pour cocktails into individual champagne flutes. (For one cocktail: Pour ½ tablespoon of elderflower syrup into a champagne flute. Add just a small amount of chilled champagne. Stir, then continue slowly pouring champagne along the inside of the side of the flute so that it does not overflow.)

CUCUMBER-INFUSED VODKA

Requires 48 hours advance preparation
Most often I like to use this vodka to make Bloody Marys. It's also fantastic served chilled, in small shot glasses.

MAKES 1 LITER
1 English cucumber, unpeeled and washed
1 liter vodka

Cut the cucumber into thirds crosswise, then cut each third in half lengthwise and each half into 6 long slices. Place the slices in a nonreactive 2-quart container. Pour in the vodka, saving the bottle. Cover the mixture and refrigerate for 48 hours.

Remove the container from refrigerator. Using tongs or a slotted spoon, remove and discard the cucumbers. Using a funnel, pour the vodka back into the vodka bottle. Put in a stopper and freeze until ready to use. The vodka can be stored for up to 1 month in the freezer.

MAKER'S MARK SOUR MADE WITH MEYER LEMON JUICE

MAKES 1 COCKTAIL

Ice

3 ounces Maker's Mark bourbon

Juice of 1 Meyer lemon

1 tablespoon confectioners' sugar

1 sour cherry, for garnish

This drink is a crowd pleaser. I get more requests for this than any other cocktail I have ever served. It is refreshing and the Maker's Mark bourbon has a wonderful finish that cuts through the sweet citrus. If you do not have Meyer lemons, use regular lemons. Depending on the size of your cocktail shaker, this recipe can be doubled or tripled. (See Sources for Meyer lemons and sour cherry).

Fill a cocktail shaker with ice. Add the bourbon, Meyer lemon juice, and confectioners' sugar. Shake well, and serve in a short-stemmed chilled glass. Garnish with the cherry.

LORA'S PUERTO RICAN EGGNOG

MAKES 5 QUARTS (32 1½-OUNCE SERVINGS)

12 egg yolks

5 12-ounce cans evaporated milk

2 teaspoons ground cinnamon

¼ teaspoon ground nutmeg

¼ teaspoon ground allspice

2 15-ounce cans cream of coconut

4 14-ounce cans sweetened condensed milk

1 bottle (750 ml) rum del Barrilito

When I was visiting Puerto Rico, my friend, Alfredo Ayala, who owns several restaurants on the island, poured me a drink after dinner. After the first sip I was addicted. He called it a "Puerto Rican Eggnog." The combination of evaporated, condensed, and coconut milks along with the various spices created a tropical version of the holiday classic.

I recommend using four-star Rum Del Barrilito (see Sources), which has a rustic woody flavor and a wonderful earthy finish. Of course, you can substitute any dark rum. This is not exactly Alfredo's recipe, but I must say it comes pretty close. It also makes a fine gift to bring to friends during the season. Serve very chilled.

In a large double-broiler, whisk together the egg yolks, evaporated milk, cinnamon, nutmeg, and allspice. Bring to a boil over medium-high heat. Stir the mixture until it reaches 160 degrees, then remove it from the heat and place the top of the double boiler in a bowl of ice, stirring until the mixture has cooled.

In a separate bowl, beat the cream of coconut with an electric mixer until smooth. Add the sweetened condensed milk and the rum and beat well. Then blend in the egg yolk mixture. Refrigerate for 24 hours up or to 1 month. Serve in chilled shot glasses or those that have been sitting in a bed of crushed ice.

DRIED ORGANIC APRICOTS WITH MARCONA ALMONDS

Marcona almonds are a staple in my pantry. They are grown in Valencia, Spain. Oval and flat, they have a higher fat content than most almonds. Although they are available raw, I prefer to buy them already roasted in olive oil and salt. I serve them along with dried apricots at my cocktail parties (see Sources).

ORANGE MARMALADE AND FRESH RICOTTA CHEESE ON AK MAK CRACKERS

Again, a great combination of ingredients to put out on a platter for guests to help themselves (see Sources).

Spread a cracker generously with ricotta cheese. Spoon 1 tablespoon of orange marmalade on the cheese and serve immediately.

DATES WITH AGED MANCHEGO CHEESE

If you are ambitious you can pit the dates and then stuff them with several small slices of manchego. Otherwise just pile some dates on a platter, and add slices of manchego. Since most aged manchego is firm, and difficult to cut, I prefer slicing it in advance.

ROSEMARY-AND-ORANGE CURED OLIVES

Stir together all the ingredients in a 12-inch skillet. Cover over medium heat for about 5 minutes, stirring occasionally, or until the olives are heated through. Remove from the heat and transfer to a serving bowl. Serve warm. (The olives can be refrigerated for up to 1 month; reheat before serving.)

MAKES 1 POUND

1 pound picholine olives, or any small green olive

3 4-inch sprigs fresh rosemary

4 4-inch long pieces of orange (or lemon) zest

2 cloves garlic, peeled and crushed

⅓ cup extra virgin olive oil

1 teaspoon sea salt

Freshly ground black pepper to taste

OYSTER SHOOTERS WITH TABASCO AND GINGER VODKA

Requires 48 hours advance preparation if making ginger vodka

When I serve oyster shooters at my cocktail parties, I prepare them throughout the evening. It is also a time I can use my mesh oyster glove (see Sources), which protects my hand while opening them. I try not to open the oysters too far in advance, but if I am having a lot of guests, I open them and store them in a small bowl on ice with their juices. To serve, I just spoon them out with a little of the juice.

Ginger infused in vodka is wonderful to drink in the winter months—the ginger warms your body. When used in the oyster shooters, it adds a special kick that everyone loves, but you can use regular vodka if you like. Just keep the vodka frozen until serving. The oyster shooters should be served very chilled.

MAKE THE GINGER VODKA: Peel the ginger, then slice crosswise into $1/8$-inch pieces. Place the slices in a nonreactive 2-quart container. Pour in the vodka, saving the bottle. Cover the mixture and refrigerate for 48 hours.

Remove the container from refrigerator. Using tongs or a slotted spoon remove and discard the ginger. Using a funnel, pour the vodka back into the bottle along with several slices of ginger. Put in a stopper and freeze until ready to use. (The vodka can be stored for up to 1 month in the freezer.)

MAKE THE SHOOTERS: Fill a large serving bowl with crushed ice. For each shooter, shuck an oyster and pour it and its juices into a small shot glass. Place the glass in the bowl of crushed ice. Repeat with all the oysters.

Pour 1 tablespoon of the ginger vodka into each shot glass. Add several drops of Tabasco sauce, a splash of lemon juice, and a chervil sprig. Serve immediately from the bowl of crushed ice.

MAKES 12 SHOOTERS

GINGER VODKA
1/2 pound fresh ginger
1 liter vodka

SHOOTERS
Crushed ice
12 small to medium oysters, such as Fanny Bay (see Sources)
Tabasco sauce
Freshly squeezed lemon juice
12 sprigs fresh chervil

STEAMED SWEET RICE WITH CAVIAR

Requires 2 hour advance preparation

MAKES 26 1-OUNCE SERVINGS

1 cup sweet rice

3 cups boiling water

7 ounces Beluga or Osetra Caviar (see Sources)

This was a course served to me at a Kaiseki dinner prepared by Yoshi-hiro Murata at Chateau de Saran, hosted by Dom Perignon. The wine-maker, Richard Geoffroy, is passionate about Japanese food paired with champagne. This combination was one of the most interesting vehicles for caviar I have ever tasted. It won't work with the champagne and elderflower cocktail, so this is the time to bring out the Dom Perignon. I make the rice several times throughout the evening dur-ing my cocktail parties so the rice is always served warm. Sweet rice will not work in an automatic rice cooker.

Soak the rice in water for 1 hour then drain in a collander. Place a steamer basket in a 4-quart casserole and line the steamer basket with several layers of cheesecloth. Spread the rice evenly over the cheese-cloth. Bring the water to a boil, reduce the heat to a medium-high simmer, cover, and steam for 20 minutes. Pour 1 ½ cups boiling water over the rice and steam for 20 minutes. Use a wooden spoon to gently break up and toss the rice after each addition. Cook about 20 minutes longer until the rice is completely transparent and sticky. Remove from the heat. Lift the cheesecloth with the rice into a bowl and cover the bowl with a kitchen towel until ready to use. It is best to serve the rice right away.

To serve, spoon a heaping tablespoon of rice into a small bowl. Top with a teaspoon of caviar. Serve immediately.

SMOKED SALMON ON NINE-GRAIN BREAD WITH DILL BUTTER

MAKES 24 FINGER SANDWICHES

4 tablespoons unsalted butter, softened

12 slices ½-inch-thick nine-grain bread or brown bread, each slice approximately 3½ by 3½

¾ pound smoked salmon, thinly sliced

4 sprigs fresh dill

The quality of the three ingredients is paramount in this very simple hors d'oeurve. First, I use a dense, rich, and very fresh nine-grain bread and slice it ½ inch thick. If the bread is not fresh, I toast it. Second, I use an unsalted French or Danish butter because they are higher in fat than most American butters and have more flavor. Finally, I use the best smoked salmon (see Sources).

Spread 1 teaspoon of the sweet butter on each slice of bread. Top all the buttered bread with smoked salmon. Slice each open face sand-wich in half diagonally and place the triangles on a platter. Top with the dill sprigs.

EDAMAME TOSSED WITH SEA SALT

Requires 2 hour advance preparation

Edamame is the Japanese name for green soy beans. You can usually find them in Japanese or Asian grocery stores. It's great to have a couple of bags in your freezer when you need last minute hors d'oeuvres.

In a large saucepan of boiling, salted water add the frozen edamame, cover, and return to a boil. Cook for 2 minutes. Using a strainer, remove the edamame from the boiling water and place them in the ice water for 2 minutes.

Drain the edamame into a colander, and shake off any excess water. Line a bowl with a kitchen towel, place the colander with the edamame in the bowl, and refrigerate uncovered for 2 hours. Before serving, remove the towel and toss the edamame with the salt.

MAKES 10 CUPS

2 20-ounce packages frozen edamame

2 teaspoons sea salt

CHOCOLATE AND ORANGE POT DE CRÉME

Requires 2 hour advance preparation

I love to make pot de créme in individual ramekins, and for years I have collected small ovenproof demitasse cups for just this occasion. Mixed and matched ramekins and demitasse cups look great passed on trays.

Orange is the only essence I like with chocolate. I use Valrhona's Noir Orange Chocolate (see Sources) and extra orange zest to provide an even more robust orange flavor.

Preheat the oven to 300 degrees. In a double boiler, melt the chocolate, heavy cream, and milk, stirring occasionally. Do not let the chocolate mixture get too hot. Once melted, remove from the heat and stir in 2 tablespoons of the sugar until dissolved.

Using an electric mixer, beat the egg yolks and remaining 2 tablespoons sugar until thick and pale, about 2 minutes. Stir in the orange zest and then $^{1}/_{2}$ cup of the chocolate mixture until well incorporated. Slowly add the remainder of the chocolate mixture and mix thoroughly.

Bring a kettle of water to a boil. Divide the chocolate mixture among 9 4- to 5-ounce ramekins or ovenproof cups. Place the ramekins or cups in a 12-by-9-inch baking pan and add boiling water to come half-way up the sides of the ramekins. Carefully place the pan in the oven and bake for 35 minutes, or until the edges of the custards are firm but the centers are still a bit soft and jiggly. Remove from the oven, and let cool. Refrigerate for several hours or up to several days before serving.

SERVES 9

4 ounces Valrhona Noir Orange chocolate, chopped

1 cup heavy cream

1 cup whole milk

4 tablespoons sugar

4 egg yolks

Finely grated zest of one orange (about 1 tablespoon)

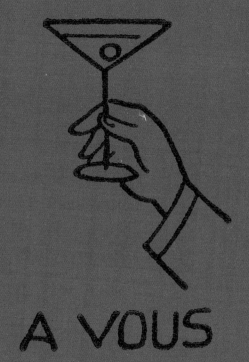

A VOUS

A New Year's Day!

NORTH CAROLINA PULLED PORK BARBECUE

BLACK-EYED PEAS WITH COLLARD GREENS

COLESLAW

PATRICK'S GILDED BOURBON-GLAZED GINGER CAKE

Worrying about my expectations for a New Year on the last day of the old one is really just too much for me. Every New Year's Eve, I feel like the day of reckoning is approaching and I wonder how I will stay awake until 12:01. All I want to do is raise my head off my pillow at 11:59 and say a little prayer. Well, my solution is to celebrate the New Year the next day when I enter it well rested. It is so comforting to get together with friends and entertain on New Year's Day and have a meal that lasts all day long.

Since I am superstitious, I figure I might as well eat foods that are supposed to bring me good luck. Every country has its own traditions for seeing in the New Year. In Japan, eating noodles in a Buddhist Temple is customary, in China you never eat fresh bean curd or tofu because it is white and unlucky, yet dried bean curd brings wealth and happiness. The Dutch eat Olie Bollen, a donutlike fritter, for good fortune. The Italians eat lentils with a pig's foot, and the French (you have to love them) often bring a jar of candied chestnuts in syrup as a gift.

Since I am an American, I am partial to the good-luck recipes of the old South. So every New Year's when I am not traveling, I cook all or part of this menu: Black eyed peas for plenty of luck, greens for plenty of money, and cabbage for additional prosperity.

NORTH CAROLINA PULLED PORK BARBECUE

SERVED 6 TO 8

PORK

3 ½ pounds pork butt, bone removed,
left whole

6 cloves garlic, peeled

1 cup apple cider vinegar

1 tablespoon freshly ground dried chilies

4 quarts cold water

Boiling water

MOPPING SAUCE

6 garlic cloves that cooked with the pork

1 teaspoon coarse salt

1½ cups pork-simmering liquid

⅓ cup cider vinegar

1 tablespoon brown sugar

Freshly ground black pepper to taste

MIXING SAUCE

½ cup pork-simmering liquid

⅓ cup store-bought smoky-flavored
barbecue sauce (not too sweet)

Sea salt to taste

Hot pepper sauce, for serving

Requires 4 hours advance preparation

PREPARE THE PORK: Place the pork, garlic, cider vinegar, and ground chilies in a 6-quart stockpot or enameled casserole.

Add the cold water and bring to a boil over high heat. Reduce the heat, partially cover, and simmer for 2½ hours, adding boiling water if necessary to keep the meat covered in the cooking liquid.

Remove the pork from the pot, and place the meat in a large roasting pan. Reserve the cooked garlic cloves and 1½ cups of the pork-simmering liquid for the mopping sauce and ½ cup liquid for the Mixing Sauce.

MAKE THE MOPPING SAUCE: Preheat the oven to 350 degrees. Mash the reserved cooked garlic cloves with the salt in a large bowl. Add the reserved 1½ cups pork-simmering liquid, the cider vinegar, brown sugar, and pepper, and mix well.

Set aside half of the mopping sauce to be used in the mixing sauce. Pour the remaining mopping sauce over the pork and baste the pork using a large pastry brush. Place it in the oven, reduce the heat to 300 degrees and cook for 1½ hours, basting every 30 minutes and turning the pork over once or twice while it is roasting. The pork should be a little crusty on the outside and very tender and moist inside.

Remove the pork from the oven and transfer it to a large chopping board to cool. Do not wash out the pot. When the pork has cooled, shred the pork finely, with your fingers. Discard any excess fat. Transfer the shredded pork to a large bowl and cover it loosely to keep it warm and moist.

MAKE THE MIXING SAUCE: Place the empty, unwashed roasting pan over very low heat and add the reserved ½ cup mopping sauce. Scrape the pan to loosen the browned bits and caramelized juices. Add the reserved 1/2 cup pork-simmering liquid. Stir in the barbecue sauce and season with salt. This Mixing Sauce will mellow considerably as the barbecue "ripens."

Add half the mixing sauce to the chopped pork and mix well. Gradually stir in the remaining mixing sauce. Cover tightly and refrigerate for at least 12 hours to let the flavor develop. (The pork can be prepared in advance and refrigerated for up to 2 days, or frozen for up to 2 months.)

Let the meat return to room temperature. Reheat, covered, in a preheated 300 degree oven. Adjust the seasonings and serve hot.

BLACK-EYED PEAS WITH COLLARD GREENS

Requires 5 hours advance preparation

Normally I add a ham hock to this recipe, but since the North Carolina Barbecue is so rich, I add wakame instead. Wakame is a dried sea vegetable that adds a hearty flavor to the beans. It is available in most health food stores. These beans develop more flavor if made the day before.

Soak the peas in a large bowl of water for 4 hours or overnight. The water should cover the peas by at least 3 inches. Remove any particles that float to the top. Rinse the peas in a colander.

Heat the olive oil in a 4-quart stockpot, add the onions, carrots, and celery, and cook until the vegetables are slightly wilted, 2 to 3 minutes. Add the black-eyed peas, water, garlic, tomatoes, cloves, bay leaf, wakame, and 2 teaspoons salt. Bring to a boil, reduce the heat, and simmer for 45 minutes or until the peas are tender.

When the beans have cooked, remove the wakame and bay leaf and stir in the collard greens. Cook for 25 minutes over low heat, adding an additional ¼ to ½ cup water if necessary to keep the beans moist. Add the red wine vinegar, and season with salt and pepper to taste.

SERVES 8 TO 10

½ *pound black-eyed peas (about 1½ cups)*

2 *tablespoons extra-virgin olive oil*

1 *medium onion, diced (about 1 cup)*

2 *medium carrots, peeled and cut into thin slices (about 1 cup)*

1 *stalk celery, finely diced (about ½ cup)*

2 *quarts cold water*

2 *cloves garlic peeled and sliced in half lengthwise*

½ *cup canned whole peeled tomatoes with their juice*

6 *whole cloves, coarsely ground in a spice grinder, or mortar and pestle*

1 *bay leaf*

½ *ounce whole dried wakame*

2 *teaspoons sea salt, plus more for seasoning*

1 *pound collard greens, washed, stalks removed, and leaves sliced crosswise into ½ inch strips*

2 *tablespoons red wine vinegar*

Freshly ground black pepper

COLESLAW

Requires 3 hours advance preparation

PREPARE THE VEGETABLES: Toss the cabbage in a bowl with the salt. Then place in a colander set over a bowl. Set aside uncovered, tossing occasionally, until the cabbage wilts, 2 to 4 hours. Rinse the cabbage under cold water. Shake out any excess water and gently pat dry with paper towels.

Place the cabbage in a serving bowl and add the carrot. Toss well.

MAKE THE DRESSING: Combine all the ingredients in a jar and shake vigorously. Add the dressing to the cabbage-carrot mixture and mix well. Cover and refrigerate for 1 hour before serving. (The coleslaw can be refrigerated for up to 2 days.)

SERVES 6 TO 8

VEGETABLES

1 *small cabbage (about 2 pounds), cored and finely shredded*

2 *teaspoons sea salt*

1 *large carrot, peeled and finely shredded*

DRESSING

½ *cup mayonnaise*

¼ *cup freshly squeezed lime juice*

2 *small serrano chiles, seeded and minced*

1 *clove garlic, finely minced*

2 *tablespoons Dijon mustard*

2 *tablespoons chopped fresh dill*

1 *tablespoon sherry vinegar*

1 *tablespoon brown sugar*

1 *teaspoon celery seeds*

1 *teaspoon sea salt*

PATRICK'S GILDED BOURBON-GLAZED GINGER CAKE

SERVES 6 TO 8

GINGER CAKE

1 ½ cups all-purpose flour,
plus more for dusting

1 teaspoon baking soda

¼ teaspoon salt

1 stick (4 ounces) unsalted butter,
plus more for greasing

¼ cup heavy cream

½ cup packed dark brown sugar

½ cup molasses

3 eggs

¼ cup finely grated fresh ginger

BOURBON GLAZE

½ cup packed dark brown sugar

½ cup Maker's Mark bourbon

3 sheets of edible gold leaf paper
(optional); (see Sources)

WHIPPED CREAM

1 cup heavy cream, chilled

1 tablespoon superfine sugar

I created this recipe because I wanted a simple yet rich cake infused with ginger and a hit of bourbon to remind me of the South.

While we were photographing this book, my friend Patrick Kinmonth gilded the cake with gold leaf. Since New Year's is about old and new traditions, this cake is now called Patrick's Gilded Boubon-Glazed Ginger Cake. We all felt it would be nice to end the year and the book with this very elegant and simple dessert.

MAKE THE GINGER CAKE: Preheat the oven to 350 degrees. Butter and flour a 9-inch cake pan. Sift together the flour, baking soda, and salt. Reserve.

Melt the butter with the heavy cream in a small saucepan. Remove from the heat and reserve.

Using an electric mixer beat the brown sugar and molasses until well blended. Add the eggs one at a time. Add the melted butter mixture and then the dry ingredients and mix well. Stir in the ginger.

Pour the batter into the baking pan and bake for 25 to 30 minutes or until a cake tester inserted in the center comes out dry. Remove the cake from the oven and prepare the bourbon glaze immediately.

MAKE THE BOURBON GLAZE: Put the brown sugar and bourbon in a small saucepan and heat over medium-high heat, stirring, until the sugar dissolves. If you're gilding the cake, brush all but ¼ cup of the glaze evenly over the whole cake while the cake is still warm. If you're not gilding the cake use all of the glaze. Let the cake rest for 2 hours before serving.

GILD THE CAKE: Using a wide gilding brush or wide pastry brush pick up a sheet of edible gold leaf and lay it across the top of the cake. Continue with several more sheets, laying them randomly across the top of the cake. Brush the reserved bourbon glaze over the top of the edible gold leaf.

MAKE THE WHIPPED CREAM: Combine the heavy cream and sugar in a large bowl. Whisk or beat until the cream is thick and forms stiff peaks. Serve with the ginger cake.

METRIC CONVERSION CHART

VOLUME EQUIVALENTS

These are not exact equivalents for American cups and spoons, but have been rounded up or down slightly to make measuring easier.

AMERICAN	METRIC	IMPERIAL
$^1/_4$ t	1.2 ml	
$^1/_2$ t	2.5 ml	
1 t	5.0 ml	
$^1/_2$ T (1.5 t)	7.5 ml	
1 T (3 t)	15 ml	
$^1/_4$ cup (4 T)	60 ml	2 fl oz
$^1/_3$ cup (5 T)	75 ml	2$^1/_2$ fl oz
$^1/_2$ cup (8 T)	125 ml	4 fl oz
$^2/_3$ cup (10 T)	150 ml	5 fl oz
$^3/_4$ cup (12 T)	175 ml	6 fl oz
1 cup (16 T)	250 ml	8 fl oz
1 $^1/_4$ cups	300 ml	10 fl oz ($^1/_2$ pt)
1 $^1/_2$ cups	350 ml	12 fl oz
2 cups (1 pint)	500 m	16 fl oz
2 $^1/_2$ cups	625 ml	20 fl oz (1 pint)
1 quart	1 liter	32 fl oz

OVEN TEMPERATURE EQUIVALENTS

OVEN MARK	F	C	GAS
VERY COOL	250-275	130-40	$^1/_2$–1
COOL	300	150	2
WARM	325	170	3
MODERATE	350	180	4
MODERATELY HOT	375	190	5
	400	200	6
HOT	425	220	7
	450	230	8
VERY HOT	475	250	9

WEIGHT EQUIVALENTS

The metric weights given in this chart are not exact equivalents, but have been rounded up or down slightly to make measuring easier.

AVOIRDUPOIS	METRIC
$^1/_4$ oz	7 g
$^1/_2$ oz	15 g
1 oz	30 g
2 oz	60 g
3 oz	90 g
4 oz	115 g
5 oz	150 g
6 oz	175 g
7 oz	200 g
8 oz ($^1/_2$ lb)	225 g
9 oz	250 g
10 oz	300 g
11 oz	325 g
12 oz	350 g
13 oz	375 g
14 oz	400 g
15 oz	425 g
16 oz (1 lb)	450 g
1$^1/_2$ lb	750 g
2 lb	900 g
2$^1/_4$ lb	1 kg
3 lb	1.4 kg
4 lb	1.8 kg

SOURCES

BAKING AND PASTRY

Chocosphere
877-922-4629
www.chocosphere.com
Valrohna chocolate and cocoa powder

THE BAKER'S CATALOGUE
135 Route 5 South
P.O. Box 876
Norwich, VT 05055
800-827-6836
www.bakerscatalogue.com

BEANS

PHIPPS COUNTRY STORE AND FARM
2700 Pescadero Road
Pescadero, CA 94060
650-879-0787
www.phippscountry.com
Over 100 varieties of heirloom and pesti-cide-free dried beans including flageolet and black-eyed peas

BREADS

POILÂNE
8 rue du Cherche-Midi
Paris 75006
011-33-1-45-48-42-59
www.poilane.fr

BREAD BAKERS GUILD OF AMERICA
www.bbga.org
Check for bakeries in your area

CAVIAR

CAVIAR RUSSE
538 Madison Avenue
New York, NY 10022
800-NY-CAVIAR
www.caviarrusse.com
Beluga and Golden Osetra Caviar

CHARCOAL

TASTE O' TEXAS
211 East Country Road 7110
Lubbock, TX 79404
806-745-4973
www.texas-mesquite.com
Organic mesquite charcoal

CHEESE & DAIRY

ARTISAN CHEESE
2413 California Street
San Francisco, CA 94115
415-929-8610
www.cowgirlcreamery.com
Comté (winter), Teleme, and Jean d'Alos cheese selections

BELLWETHER FARMS
999 Valley Ford Road
Petaluma, CA 94952
888-527-8606
www.bellwethercheese.com
Cow's and sheeps milk ricotta

COWGIRL CREAMERY
P.O. Box 594
80 Fourth St.
Point Reyes Station, CA 94956
415-663-9335
www.cowgirlcreamery.com
Artisanal cheese selections

JOE'S DAIRY
156 Sullivan Street
New York, NY 10012
212-677-8780
Fresh mozzarella

MURRAY'S CHEESE SHOP
257 Bleecker Street
New York, NY 10014
888-MY-CHEEZ
www.murrayscheese.com
Sheep's milk ricotta, mascarpone, fromage blanc, Roquefort, farmer's cheese, Parmigiano, and Pecorino. Seasonally: Munster, Cabéciou de Rocamadour, and Vacherin

PELUSO CHEESE
429 H Street
Los Banos, CA 93635
209-826-3744
Teleme

STRAUS FAMILY CREAMERY
P.O. Box 768
Marshall, CA 94940
415-663-5464
www.strausmilk.com
Organic unsalted sweet and salted butter, milk, and yogurt

VERMONT BUTTER & CHEESE
COMPANY
40 Pitman Road
Websterville, VT 05678
800-884-6287
www.vtbutterandcheeseco.com
Cultured butter with 86% butterfat

FARMER'S MARKETS

www.ams.usda.gov/farmersmarkets

FISH AND SHELLFISH

MCLAUGHLIN'S SEAFOOD
728 Main Street
Bangor, ME 04401
800-222-9107
Lobster available by mail order

SWAN OYSTER DEPOT
1517 Polk Street
San Francisco, CA 94109
415-673-1101
Oysters, Dungeness crab, and smoked salmon

UNIVERSITY SEAFOOD & POULTRY CO.
1317 North East 47th Street
Seattle, WA 98105
206-632-3700
Dungeness crab, oysters, and wild salmon (seasonal)

FOIE GRAS AND POULTRY

D'ARTAGNAN
280 Wilson Avenue
Newark, NJ 07105
800-327-8246
www.dartagnan.com
Fresh and cooked foie gras, Guinea hen, pheasant, Muscovy duck breasts, and turkey

GRIMAUD FARMS OF CALIFORNIA
1320-A South Aurora
Stockton, CA 95206
800-466-9955
www.grimaud.com
Muscovy duck breast, Guinea hen, and specialty poultry

HUDSON VALLEY FOIE GRAS
80 Brooks Road
Ferndale, NY 12734
845-292-2500
www.hudsonvalleyfoiegras.com

LES PRODUITS JEAN LEGRAND
11, rue Pierre Demones
750017 Paris
011-33-1-40-55-92-20
Fresh foie gras

FRUITS AND VEGETABLES

AGATA & VALENTINA
1505 First Ave.
New York, NY 10021
212-452-0690
La Ratte de Paris potatoes (seasonal)

FROG HOLLOW FARM
P.O. Box 872
Brentwood, CA 94513
888-779-4511
www.froghollow.com
Organic O'Henry and Cal Red peaches (seasonal)

HONEYCRISP
9400 South Lac Jac
Reedly, CA 93654
877-638-3084
Meyer lemons (seasonal)

JERZY BOYZ
509-682-6269
www.jerzyboyz.com
Organic apples and pears (seasonal)

KATZ AND COMPANY
101 South Coombs, Suite Y-3
Napa, CA 94559
800-676-7176
www.katzandco.com
Meyer lemons (seasonal)

GRITS

ANSON MILLS
1922 C Gervais Street
Columbia, SC 29201
803-467-4122 (by appointment)
www.ansonmillls.com
Organic stone ground grits

KITCHEN EQUIPMENT

BASS PRO SHOPS OUTDOORS
800-227-7776
www.basspro.com
*Eight-quart outdoor fish cooker with
cast-iron Dutch oven*

BROADWAY PANHANDLER
477 Broome Street
New York, NY 10013
866-COOKWARE
www.broadwaypanhandler.com

BRIDGE KITCHENWARE
214 East 52nd Street
New York, NY 10022
212-688-4220
www.bridgekitchenware.com
*Copper tart tatin mold, truffle shaver,
and crème brûlée molds*

E. DEHILLERIN
18 & 20, rue Coquillière
51, rue Jean-Jacques Rousseau
75001 Paris
011-44-1-42-36-53-13
www.e-dehillerin.fr
*Potato ricer, copper tart tatin molds,
and oyster trays for serving*

THE GARDENER
1836 Fourth Street
Berkeley, CA 94710
510-548-4545
www.thegardener.com
Tuscan grill

G. LORENZI
Via Montenapoleone, 9
20121 Milan, Italy
011-39-02-760-228-48
www.glorenzi.com
*Ceramic knife, mesh oyster glove, and
peppermill for dried red chilies*

STAUB
866-STAUB-US

Sur La Table
84 Pine Street
Seattle, WA 98101
800-243-0852
www.surlatable.com
*Butane torch, Microplane graters, and
marble mortar and pestle*

MEAT

BELLOTA-BELLOTA
18, rue Jean Nicot
75007 Paris
011-33-1-53-59-96-96
Artisanal Iberian ham

FLORENCE PRIME MEAT MARKET
5 Jones Street
New York, NY 10014
212-242-6531
Prime dry aged porterhouse steak

FLYING PIGS FARM
246 Sutherland Road
Shushan, NY 12873
518-854-3844
www.flyingpigsfarm.com
Pork and smoked bacon

JAMISON FARM
171 Jamison Lane
Latrobe, PA 15650
800-237-5262
www.jamisonfarm.com
Lamb

HOBBS APPLEWOOD SMOKED MEATS
1201 Anderson Drive #H
San Raphael, CA 94901
415-453-0577
Bacon, Speck Ham

MUSHROOMS

MARCHE AUX DELICES
P.O. Box 1164
New York, NY 10028
888-547-5471
www.auxdelices.com
Morels and porcini

NUTS

TIENDA.COM
108-16 Ingram Road
Williamsburg, VA 23188
888-472-1022
www.tienda.com
Marcona almonds

SPECIALTY FOOD STORES

BENDICKS BITTERMINTS
www.britstore.co.uk

DEAN & DELUCA
560 Broadway
New York, NY 10012
800-999-0306
www.deananddeluca.com

FOUQUET
36, rue Laffitte
75009 Paris
011-33-1-47-70-85-00
22 rue François
75008 Paris
011-33-1-47-23-30-36
www.fouquet.fr
*Fleur de sel, peppercorns with spices,
lavender honey, and sour cherries*

JUNE TAYLOR COMPANY
510-923-1522
www.junetaylorjams.com
Orange marmalade

KALUSTYAN'S
123 Lexington Avenue
New York, NY 10016
800-352-3451
www.kalustyans.com
*Indian spices, kaffir lime leaves, curry
leaves, ghee, yogurt, tamarind paste,
split red lentils, black mustard seeds,
and Iranian saffron*

MANICARETTI
888-952-4005
www.manicaretti.com
*Importer of Italian food; Rustichella
d'Abruzzo pasta (Garganelle), aborio
rice, balsamic vinegar, chickpea flour,
and olive oil*

CLARKE'S
122 Kensington Church Street
London, England W8 4BH
011-44-207-229-2190
www.sallyclarke.com
Elderflower syrup

SEA STAR SEA SALT
P.O. Box 55
Oakville, CA 94562
888-767-SALT
www.seastarseasalt.com

TRUFFLES

DA ROSARIO
29-24 40th Avenue
Long Island City, NY 11101
800-281-2330
Black truffles (seasonal)

PEBEYRE
66, rue Frédéric-Suisse
4600 Cahors, France
011-44-5-65-22-24-80
info@pebeyre.fr
Black truffles (seasonal)

VINTAGE COOKING EQUIPMENT

LUCULLUS
610 Chartres Street
New Orleans, LA 70130
504-528-9620
*Vintage French cooking vessels,
mortars, and tabletop items*

WINES

E&R WINE SHOP
6141 SW Macadam
Portland, OR 97239
877-410-8654
*Fantastic selection of Italian wines,
including Moscato d'Asti and Arneis*

KERMIT LYNCH WINE MERCHANT
1605 San Pablo Avenue
Berkeley, CA 94702
510-524-1524
*Domaine Zind Humbrecht and
Domaine Tempier Bandol Rosé*

PREMIER CRU
5890 Christie Avenue
Emeryville, CA 94608
510-655-6691
www.premiercru.net
Great selection of difficult-to-find wines

SAM'S WINE WAREHOUSE
Sam's Wine & Spirits
1720 North Marcey Street
Chicago, IL 60614
866-SAMSWINE
www.samswine.com
*They have almost all my favorite wines,
including the Castello di Monsanto's
Chianti*

MISCELLANEOUS

PEARL PAINT
308 Canal Street
New York, NY 10013
www.pearlpaint.com
Edible gold leaf

NANDINI INC.
Theraputic grade essential oils
845-434-2408
Nandiniyes@hotmail.com
*Full line of theraputic grade essential
oils, including geranium oil*

ACKNOWLEDGMENTS

If there is a thread that holds this book together, it is that of love, so in expressing my gratitude I want to begin by thanking my father, Peter Zarubin, a single parent who raised three children and still managed to put fresh food on the table at every meal.

I feel equally blessed by the tangible and intangible contributions of friends and colleagues, beginning with Tessa Traeger who brought my love of food to life with her magical photographs. Thank you, Tessa for all your ideas along the way and for encouraging me to be me and to take my own risks. And thank you Tessa and Patrick for your hospitality at Corey Manor, the most beautiful possible setting for our work together.

Gorgeous photographs and delicious recipes would be lost without a brilliant design to do them justice. Thank you Anne Johnson, for all that you did to help shape, direct, and produce the look of this book. And thank you for believing and supporting me even before there was a book; the simplicity of your ideas helped me keep it in focus.

Mia Bremridge's assistance went far beyond my expectations. Thank you Mia, for all the driving, for the late nights, for always having a pot of tea ready at the perfect moment and for the laborious task of writing the "May I?" instructions. And thanks also to Andrew Jewels who leant a hand whenever it was needed. To Peter Dixon and Steve de Wet who so ably assist Tessa, thank you too. And to Zoe Harris and Michelle Ingram, I am so grateful for your support.

To my friend and editor at *House & Garden* magazine, Dominique Browning, my thanks for giving me the greatest job in the world and for your guidance over the years. And, of course, thank you for introducing me to Jay McInerney.

Then there are the words. Thank you, Elizabeth Pochoda, for helping me make my words stand on their feet and for your dedication to them.

If it weren't for Gail Monaghan, my tireless editor who worked with me so patiently and so long there would be no book. Thank you.

Thanks to Mark Magowan for taking me on at Abrams and to Leslie Stoker who oversaw the project at Stewart, Tabori & Chang and exerted enough calm to keep its focus and its integrity intact. And to everyone at Stewart Tabori & Chang, I appreciate all of your help.

Thank you, Jay McInerney, for being my partner in so many wonderful food and wine experiences. May we have many more opportunities to eat and drink together.

Many other people have helped me over the years. Susie Tompkins taught me about good food and the quality of a good life. She also impressed upon me the importance of visual presentation.

Dan Shaw and Lygeia Grace gave me encouragement in the early days of of this project. Brooke Collier did excellent work in helping me with the sources for the book. Thank you Mona Talbot for testing many of the recipes.

Alice Waters's strength, dedication, and consistency for more than three decades at Chez Panisse have earned the thanks of thousands including me. To all the cooks at Chez Panisse, thank you for years of delicious and inspiring food.

And special thanks to all my friends whose visual contribution to this book made it even more special. Patrick Kinmoth, Ted Muehling, Mats Gustafson, Annie Leibovitz, Brigitte Lacombe, Bruno Borie, Edith Mezard, David Mclean, Jeffrey Miller, Alberto Bianco, Anita Calero, Ann Hazu, Nina Truch, Lori Goldstein, and Muriel Grateau.

Thanks to all the dedicated growers, farmers, purveyors, and winemakers whose devotion to the integrity of the ingredients inspires me to cook. And especially to the Pebeyre family in Cahors, France, whose superb truffles are matched only by their hospitality. To everyone I have had the privilege to cook for and with, and to everyone who has cooked for me, thank all of you for the memories.

And finally, thank you to S.C., for helping me see my own worthiness and for teaching me to pass on to others what I have learned along the way.

INDEX

Trains on the Tracks

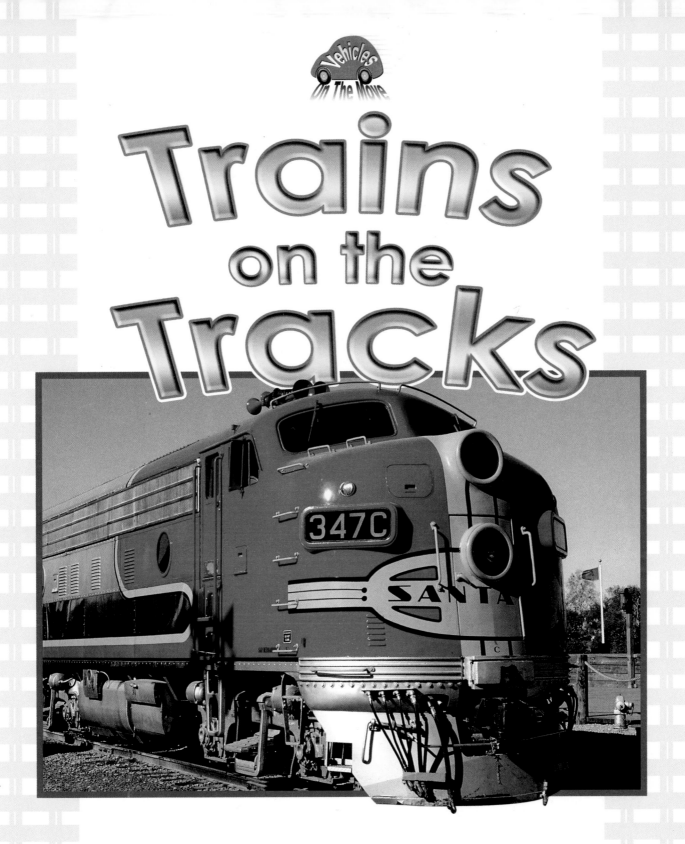

Kathryn Smithyman and Bobbie Kalman

🌲 **Crabtree Publishing Company**

www.crabtreebooks.com

Created by Bobbie Kalman

Dedicated by Bobbie Kalman
For our grandsons Sean and Liam (our two expert train engineers)

Editor-in-Chief
Bobbie Kalman

Writing team
Kathryn Smithyman
Bobbie Kalman

Substantive editor
Kelley MacAulay

Editors
Molly Aloian
Michael Hodge

Photo research
Crystal Foxton

Design
Margaret Amy Salter

Production coordinator
Heather Fitzpatrick

Prepress technician
Nancy Johnson

Consultant
Michael E. Telzrow, Executive Director
National Railroad Museum, Green Bay, Wisconsin

Special thanks to
Steve Cruickshanks (Ethan's train grandpa), Amtrak, a service mark of the National Railroad
Passenger Corp. (U.S.), Canadian National Railway, and Canadian Pacific Railway

Illustrations
Vanessa Parson-Robbs: back cover, pages 7, 9, 11, 14, 16, 17, 18, 20, 24, 27, 32 (boxcar,
    freight train, gondola car, hopper car, locomotive, passenger train, and tank car)
Margaret Amy Salter: pages 21, 31, 32 (autorack, elevated train, flat car, passenger car,
    subway, and train station)

Photographs
Amtrak, a service mark of the National Railroad Passenger Corp. (U.S.): pages 13 (top), 28
Canadian Pacific Railway: pages 5, 23, 24-25, 29 (top)
CN: page 22
Corbis: © Colin Garratt, Milepost 92 $1/2$: page 7; © Jean Heguy: pages 18-19;
    Joseph Sohm: page 27
Fotolia.com: © Wai Heng Chow: page 26; © John Stelzer: page 31
iStockphoto.com: Aback Photography: page 6; Denise Kappa: page 21; James Pauls: page 11;
    Kenneth Sponsler: page 17
© WOLFGANG KAEHLER, www.wkaehlerphoto.com: page 29 (bottom)
© Marcel Marchon: page 30
© ShutterStock.com: Anita: pages 10, 20; Mariano N. Ruiz: pages 8-9
Other images by Corel

Library and Archives Canada Cataloguing in Publication

Smithyman, Kathryn
    Trains on the tracks / Kathryn Smithyman & Bobbie Kalman.

(Vehicles on the move)
Includes index.
ISBN 978-0-7787-3045-3 (bound)
ISBN 978-0-7787-3059-0 (pbk.)

    1. Railroad trains--Juvenile literature. I. Kalman, Bobbie, 1947- II. Title.
III. Series.

TF148.S65 2007   j625.1   C2007-900946-8

Library of Congress Cataloging-in-Publication Data

Smithyman, Kathryn, 1961-
    Trains on the tracks / Kathryn Smithyman & Bobbie Kalman.
        p. cm. -- (Vehicles on the move)
    Includes index.
    ISBN-13: 978-0-7787-3045-3 (rlb)
    ISBN-10: 0-7787-3045-X (rlb)
    ISBN-13: 978-0-7787-3059-0 (pb)
    ISBN-10: 0-7787-3059-X (pb)
    1. Railroad trains--Juvenile literature. I. Kalman, Bobbie. II. Title.
TF148.S69 2007
625.2--dc22
                                                              2007005078

Crabtree Publishing Company

www.crabtreebooks.com   1-800-387-7650

Published in Canada
Crabtree Publishing
616 Welland Ave.
St. Catharines, Ontario
L2M 5V6

Published in the
United States
Crabtree Publishing
PMB16A
350 Fifth Ave., Suite 3308
New York, NY 10118

Published in the
United Kingdom
Crabtree Publishing
White Cross Mills
High Town, Lancaster
LA1 4XS

Published in Australia
Crabtree Publishing
386 Mt. Alexander Rd.
Ascot Vale (Melbourne)
VIC 3032

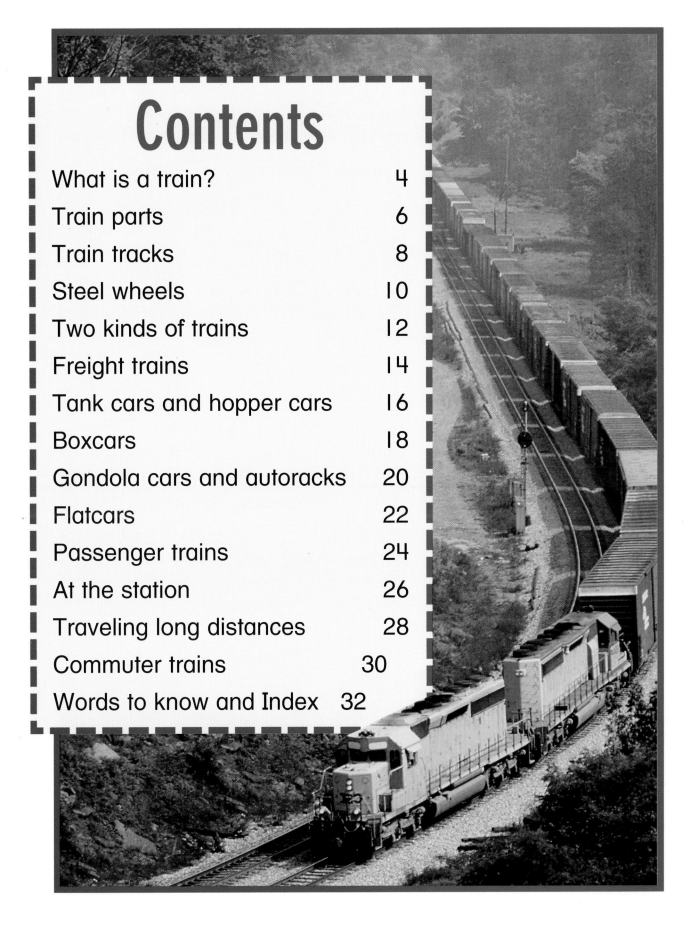

Contents

What is a train?

A **train** is a **vehicle**. A vehicle is a machine. Vehicles move from place to place. They move people and things. A train moves from place to place on **tracks**.

tracks

Parts of a train

A train has a **locomotive**. The locomotive has an **engine**. An engine gives the train **power**. Power makes the train move. A train also has **railcars**. The locomotive pulls the railcars.

railcar

locomotive

The locomotive is at the front of the train.

Train parts

Locomotives and railcars have parts called **knuckle couplers**. Knuckle couplers join railcars together. They also join railcars to locomotives.

knuckle coupler

Locomotives and railcars have knuckle couplers on their front ends. They also have knuckle couplers on their back ends.

Locomotive parts

Locomotives have parts that railcars do not have. They have **cabs**, **headlights**, and **horns**.

A locomotive's horn makes a loud noise. The noise tells people that the train is coming!

Headlights are lights on the front of the locomotive. They help the driver of the train see the tracks ahead of the train.

cab

fireman

engineer

*The driver of a train is called an **engineer**. The engineer sits on the right side of the cab. The **fireman** helps the engineer. The fireman sits on the left side of the cab.*

Train tracks

Trains travel on tracks. Most tracks
have two **rails**. Rails are long, thin
bars. They are made of **steel**. Steel is
a kind of metal. Steel is strong and hard.

rail

Ties and spikes

Rails lie on top of **ties**. Most ties are pieces of wood. **Spikes** attach the rails to the ties. Spikes are long metal nails. The spikes hold the rails in place.

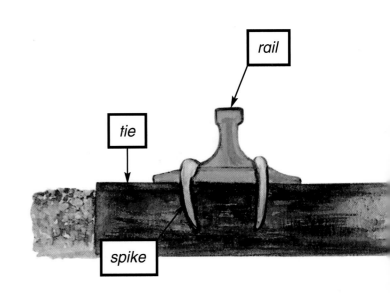

rail

tie

spike

tie

Tracks are laid on top of gravel called **ballast**.

Steel wheels

Trains move on **wheels**. The wheels are on the locomotives and the railcars. The wheels are round. They are made of steel.

wheel

A perfect fit

Each train wheel has two **rims**. A rim is the edge of a wheel. One rim of a train wheel is larger than the other rim is. The larger rim is called a **flange**. The flange holds the wheel firmly on the rail.

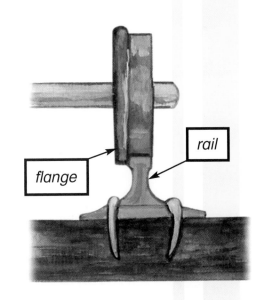

flange

rail

flange

A flange stops a train wheel from slipping off the tracks.

Two kinds of trains

There are different kinds of trains. Most trains are **freight trains**. Freight trains carry **freight**. Freight is a load of things. Freight trains carry freight in railcars. Railcars that carry freight are called **freight cars**.

freight cars

Freight trains carry many kinds of freight. Wheat, logs, and new cars are kinds of freight.

Passenger trains

Some trains are **passenger trains**. These trains carry **passengers**. Passengers are people who are riding on trains. They ride in railcars called **passenger cars**.

Passenger cars have seats in them. People sit in the seats.

passenger car

Passenger cars have windows. The passengers can look out the windows.

Freight trains

Freight trains have large, powerful
locomotives called **freight locomotives**.
Freight locomotives can pull
many freight cars
filled with freight.

Pulling partners

Sometimes freight cars carry very heavy freight. One locomotive may not be able to pull these freight cars. Two or more locomotives can be joined together. Together, these locomotives can pull very heavy freight cars.

Four freight locomotives are pulling this freight train.

Tank cars and hopper cars

Different kinds of freight cars carry different kinds of freight. **Tank cars** are freight cars. They carry liquids. Each tank car carries a different liquid. Some tank cars carry milk. Other tank cars carry **gasoline**. Gasoline is the fuel that most vehicles use for power.

tank car

Hopper cars

A **hopper car** is another kind of freight car. It can carry huge loads of sand or gravel. There are doors in the floor of a hopper car. The doors open and close. When the doors open, the load pours out. It pours out into huge metal boxes. The boxes are below the tracks.

These hopper cars are holding freight. Their doors are closed.

Boxcars

Many freight cars are **boxcars**. Boxcars carry **packaged freight**. Packaged freight is freight that is wrapped in paper or plastic. Packaged freight may also be packed in boxes. Boxcars carry packaged freight such as canned foods, televisions, or books.

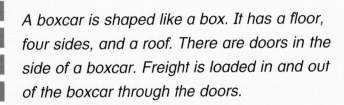

A boxcar is shaped like a box. It has a floor, four sides, and a roof. There are doors in the side of a boxcar. Freight is loaded in and out of the boxcar through the doors.

forklift

Machines called **forklifts** move freight in and out of boxcars.

Gondola cars and autoracks

A **gondola car** is another kind of freight car. It has four sides, but it does not have a roof. Gondola cars carry different kinds of freight. They may carry machine parts, scraps of metal, or logs.

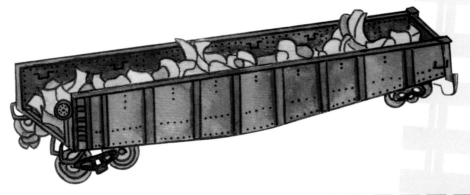

These gondola cars are carrying logs.

Autoracks

Autoracks are freight cars that carry vehicles, such as cars, vans, and trucks. To load an autorack, people drive these vehicles up a **ramp** and into the autorack.

ramp

Each autorack holds about twenty vehicles.

Flatcars

Almost all freight trains have **flatcars**. Flatcars do not have walls or roofs. Flatcars carry machines, pipes, and wood. Some of the freight that flatcars carry is huge! Huge freight is too big to fit on other kinds of freight cars.

This flatcar is carrying huge pipes.

tank

This flatcar is carring a huge **tank**!

Passenger trains

Passenger trains carry people from place to place. Each passenger car carries a lot of people. Passenger cars weigh less than freight cars do. They also move faster than freight trains. Their locomotives have less weight to pull.

At the station

Passenger trains travel to **train stations**.
People get on trains at one train station.
They get off trains at another train station.
At train stations, there are buildings where
people wait for trains to arrive.

platform

*People wait for trains on **platforms**. Trains stop next to the platforms.*

Ticket to ride

People can buy **tickets** at train stations. Each person must have a ticket to ride on a train. A **conductor** checks each passenger's ticket. The conductor checks to make sure each passenger is on the right train.

TRAIN PASSENGER TICKET

RIDERS 1

PAY CODE VI
ACC.# 243678436896

NAME OF PASSENGER: MARY SMITH
FROM New York Penn, NY
TO NEW CARROLLTON, MD
CARRIER A3
SPACE/CAR METRO COACH

RES. NO. 261678
DEPT.DATE 03APR07
TIME 0600P
DATE OF ISSUE 01APR07
TRAIN 125

RAIL FARE $79.00

Boarding Pass

Passenger Receipt
NAME OF PASSENGER: MARY SMITH
FROM New York Penn, NY
TO NEW CARROLLTON, MD
CARRIER A3   TRAIN 125
SPACE/CAR METRO COACH
DEPT. DATE 03APR07 TIME 0600P

SUBJECT TO CHANGE ON REVERSE RAIL FARE $79.00

This conductor has checked all the passengers' tickets.

Traveling long distances

Some passengers travel very long distances on trains. Traveling long distances may take days. On a long trip, passengers need places to eat and sleep. Passenger trains that carry people long distances have special cars. These pages show some of the special cars.

*Passengers eat meals in the **dining car**.*

*Passengers can sleep in a **sleeping car**. The sleeping car has beds called **berths**.*

*An **observation car** has large windows in its sides and roof. Passengers in the observation car can see mountains, lakes, and other beautiful sights from the train.*

Commuter trains

Commuter trains are passenger trains on which people travel every day. Passengers take the trains to work, to school, or to other places they need to go.

Subways

Most large cities have **subways**. Subways are commuter trains that travel under the ground.

Elevated trains

Some cities have commuter trains called **elevated trains**. Elevated trains travel on tracks high above the ground.

Elevated trains are sometimes called "els."

Words to know and Index

autorack
pages 20, 21

boxcar
pages 18-19

elevated train
page 31

flatcar
pages 22-23

freight train
pages 12, 14-15, 22, 24

gondola car
page 20

hopper car
pages 16, 17

locomotive
pages 5, 6, 7, 10, 14, 15, 24

passenger car
pages 13, 24

passenger train
pages 13, 24-25, 26, 28, 30

subway
page 31

Other index words

commuter trains 30-31
dining cars 28
observation cars 29
railcars 5, 6, 7, 10, 12, 13
sleeping cars 29
tracks 4, 7, 8-9, 11, 17, 31
wheels 10-11

tank car
page 16

train station
pages 26-27

Printed in the USA